The Romantic Tradition in American Literature

The Romantic Tradition in American Literature

Advisory Editor

HAROLD BLOOM
Professor of English, Yale University

FROISSART BALLADS,

AND

OTHER POEMS

BY

PHILIP PENDLETON COOKE

ARNO PRESS
A NEW YORK TIMES COMPANY
New York • 1972

Reprint Edition 1972 by Arno Press Inc.

Reprinted from a copy in The Princeton
University Library

The Romantic Tradition in American Literature
ISBN for complete set: 0-405-04620-0
See last pages of this volume for titles.

Manufactured in the United States of America

ෆ෧ෆ෧ෆ෧ෆ෧ෆ෧ෆ෧ෆ෧ෆ෧ෆ෧

Library of Congress Cataloging in Publication Data

Cooke, Philip Pendleton, 1816-1850.
    Froissart ballads, and other poems.

    (The Romantic tradition in American literature)
    I. Title. II. Series.
PS1387.F7 1972   811'.3   72-4959
ISBN 0-405-04631-6

FROISSART BALLADS.

FROISSART BALLADS,

OTHER POEMS.

BY

PHILIP PENDLETON COOKE.

" Emmi venuta certa fantasia,
Che non posso cacciarmi da la testa,
Di scriver un istoria in poesia
Affatta ignota o poco manifesta."

FORTEGUERRI.

PHILADELPHIA:
CAREY AND HART.
1847.

C. SHERMAN, PRINTER,

19 St. James Street.

CONTENTS.

MISCELLANEOUS POEMS.

PREFACE.

The motto of my title-page—the opening lines of the Ricciar-detto of the Roman poet and prelate, Forteguerri—gives an accurate idea of the plan of the Froissart Ballads, as I originally conceived it :

> " A certain freak has got into my head,
>   Which I can't conquer for the life of me,
> Of taking up some history, little read,
>   Or known, and writing it in poetry."

The Proem was written whilst my "freak" or purpose was still of this limited character ; and it represents the ballads—not then begun, but spoken of as finished—as versified transcripts from Froissart. Perhaps, if I had carried out this purpose of fidelity to the noble old chronicler, my poetry would have been all the better for it. I have, however, not done so. The Master of Bolton, and Geoffrey Tetenoire are no where in Froissart, but stories of my own invention. The only material aid I have drawn from his chronicles, in the first of these poems, is in the jousting scenes of its concluding parts. They are borrowed "with a difference" from his account of "the deeds of arms at St. Ingilbert, otherwise called Sandingfeld, in the justs enterprised by Sir Raynold of Roy, the young Sir Boucequant, and the Lord of Saimpi." I have also adopted my names generally from his sonorous Norman and Frank lists. The hawking incident is taken from a fine old story, by what author I do not recollect, called Love's Falconrie—an appropriation which the plan of my labours, aiming at no originality of story—was supposed to warrant. In Geoffrey Tetenoire, Froissart supplies nothing except Geoffrey himself, and the fact that he drove the Countess of Montpensier and Ventadore from her castle of Ventadore. The remaining poems, Orthone, Sir Peter of Bearn, and Our Lady's Dog, are written upon the original plan, and as faithful to the text of Froissart as the necessities of verse permitted me to make them.

The reader may be disposed to undervalue poems professing to be versifications of old stories, on the ground of a want of originality. I ask only, in anticipation of this, that he will recollect the fact that, from Chaucer to Dryden, such appropriations of old story were customary with the noblest poets of our English language. Of the Canterbury Tales of Chaucer, the plots, and even most of the incidents, of all except one or two, have been traced by Tyrwhitt and other editors to earlier (chiefly Italian) sources. Even amongst the best poets of a recent day, the practice has been to some extent retained. Until the world thinks the less of the Canterbury Tales, or of the Basil Pot of John Keats, for the fact that they trace to the Filocopo and Decameron, I shall hope to be justified in that plan of my work to which, in three poems out of five, I have adhered, and to which it is my purpose to adhere in some future poems.

In this connexion I may as well inform the reader that the ballads now published, which he may find already too numerous considering their quality, are only a few of my projected, and, in some cases, roughly-executed Froissart Ballads. The Bridge of Lusac, Mont d'Or, The Death of Young Gaston of Foix, Belleperche, and several others, are still behind. If my book lives at all beyond the present day, I may hereafter add these stories to the present list, and make the collection answer, in bulk, at least, to the somewhat over-loud note of preparation sounded in the Proem.

P. P. C.

Millwood, Clarke Co., Va.
Nov. 10, 1846.

EMILY:

A PROEM TO THE FROISSART BALLADS.

" Uprose the sun, and uprose Emily."
CHAUCER.

YOUNG EMILY has temples fair,
Caressed by locks of dark brown hair.
A thousand sweet humanities
Speak wisely from her hazel eyes.
Her speech is ignorant of command,
But it can lead you like a hand.
Her white teeth sparkle when the eclipse,
Is laughter-moved, of her red lips.
She moves—all grace—with gliding limbs,
As a white-breasted cygnet swims.

In her sweet childhood, Emily,
Was wild with natural gayety,

2

A little creature, full of laughter,
Who cast no thought before or after,
And knew not custom or its chains.
The dappled fawns upon the plains,
The birds that filled the morning skies
Above her, with their ecstacies—
Of love and music prodigal—
Were not more gladly natural.

But with this childish merriment,
Mind, and the ripening years, have blent
A thoughtfulness—not melancholy—
Which wins her life away from folly;
Checking somewhat the natural gladness,
But saved, by that it checks, from sadness—
Like clouds, across a May-morn sailing,
Which take the golden light they are veiling.
She loves her kind, and shuns no duty,
Her virtues sanctify her beauty,
And all who know her say that she
Was born for man's felicity.

I know that she was born for mine;
Dearer than any joy of wine,
Of pomp, or gold, or man's loud praise,
Or purple power, art thou to me—
Kind cheerer of my clouded ways—
Young vine upon a rugged tree!

Maidens who love are full of hope,
And crowds hedge in its golden scope;
Therefore they love green solitudes
And silence for their better moods.
I know some wilds where tulip trees,
Full of the singing toil of bees,
Depend their loving branches over
Great rocks, which honeysuckles cover
In rich and liberal overflow.
In the dear time of long ago,
When I had wooed young Emily,
And she had told her love to me,
I often found her in these bowers
Quite rapt away in meditation,
Or giving earnest contemplation
To leaf, or bird, or wild-wood flowers;

And once I heard the maiden singing,
Until the very woods were ringing—
Singing an old song to the hours!
I well remember that rare song,
It charged the hours with cruel wrong—
Wrong to the verdure of the boughs—
Wrong to the lustre of fair brows.
Its music had a wondrous sound,
And made the greenwood haunted ground.
But I delay : one jocund morn—
A morn of that blithe time of spring,
When milky blossoms load the thorn,
And birds so prate, and soar, and sing,
That melody is every where,
On the glad earth and in the air—
On such a morn I went to seek,
Through our wild haunts, for Emily.
I found her where a flowering tree
Gave odours and cool shade.   Her cheek
A little rested on her hand ;
Her rustic skill had made a band,
Of fair device, which garlanded
The beauty of her bending head ;

Some maiden thoughts, most kind and wise,
Were dimly burning in her eyes.
When I beheld her—form and face
So lithe, so fair—the spirit race,
Of whom the better poets dreamed,
Came to my thought, and I half deemed
My earth-born mistress, pure and good,
Was some such lady of the wood
As she who worked at spell and snare,
With Huon of the dusky hair,
And fled, in likeness of a doe,
Before the fleet youth Angelo.
But these infirm imaginings
Flew quite away on instant wings.
I called her name.   A swift surprise
Came whitely to her face, but soon
It fled before some daintier dyes,
And, laughing like a brook in June,
With sweet accost she welcomed me ;
And I sate there with Emily.
The gods were very good to bless
My life with so much happiness

The maiden on that lowly seat—
I sitting at her little feet!
Two happier lovers never met
In dear and talk-charmed privacy.
It was a golden day to me,
And its great bliss is with me yet,
Warming, like wine, my inmost heart—
For memories of happy hours
Are like the cordials pressed from flowers,
And madden sweetly.

                I impart
Naught of the love-talk I remember,
For May's young pleasures are best hid
From the cold prudence of December,
Which clips, and chills, all vernal wings ;
And love's own sanctities forbid,
Now, as of old, such gossippings
In hall, of what befalls in bower.
But other matters of the hour,
Of which it breaks no faith to tell,
My homely rhyme shall chronicle.

As silently we sate alone—
Our love-talk spent—two mated birds
Began to prate in loving tone ;
Quoth Emily, " They sure have words !
Didst hear them say ' *My sweet*,' ' *My dear* ?''
And as they chirped, we laughed to hear.

Soon after this a southern wind
Came sobbing, like a hunted hind,
Into the quiet of the glen.
The maiden mused awhile, and then
Worded her thought right playfully.
" These winds," she said, " of land and sea,
My friend, are surely living things
That come and go on unseen wings.
The teeming air, and prodigal,
Which droops its azure over all,
Is full of immortalities
That look on us with unseen eyes.
This sudden wind that hath come here,
With its low sobs of pain or fear,

It may be is a spirit kind
That loves the bruisèd flowers to bind,
Whose task it is to shake the dew
From the sad violet's eye of blue,
Or chase the honey-making thieves
From off the rose, and shut its leaves
Against the cold of April eves.
Perhaps its dainty, pink-tipt, hands
Have plied such tasks in far-off lands,
And now, perchance, some grim foe follows
The little wight to these green hollows."
Such gentle words had Emily
For the south wind in the tulip tree.

A runnel, hidden by the trees,
Gave out some natural melodies.
She said " The brook among the stones
Is solemn in its undertones :
How like a hymn ! the singing creature
Is worshipping the God of Nature."
But I replied, " My dear—not so ;
Thy solemn eyes, thy brow of snow,

And, more than these, thy maiden merit,
Have won Undine, that gentle spirit,
To sing her songs of love to thee."
Swift answered merry Emily,
" Undine is but a girl, you know,
And would not pine for love of me ;
She has been peering from the brook
And glimpsed at you." She said, and shook
With a rare fit of silvery laughter.
I was more circumspect thereafter,
And dealt in homelier talk. A man
May call a white-browed girl *Dian*,
But likes not to be turned upon,
And nick-named *Young Endymion*.

My Emily loved very well,
At times, those ancient lays which tell
Rude natural tales ; she had no lore
Of trouvere or of troubadour,
Nor knew what difference there might be
Between the tongues of *oc* and *oui ;*

But hearing old tales, loved them all,
If truth but made them natural,
In our good talks, we oft went o'er
The little hoard of my quaint lore,
Culled out of old melodious fable.
She little cared for Arthur's Table,
For tales of doughty Launcelot,
Or Tristram, or of him who smote
The giant, Angoulafre hight,
And moaned for love by day and night ;
She little cared for such as these.
But if I crossed the Pyrenees,
With the great peers of Charlemagne
Descending toward the Spanish plain,
Her eye would lighten at the strain.
And it would moisten with a tear.
The sad end of that tale to hear ;
How, all aweary, worn, and white,
Urging his foaming horse amain,
A courier from the south, one night,
Reached the great city of the Seine ;

And how, at that same time and hour,
The bride of Roland lay in bower,
Wakeful, and quick of ear to win
Some rumour of her Paladin—
And how it came, in sudden cries
That shook the earth, and rent the skies;
And how the messenger of fate—
The courier who rode so late—
Was dragged on to her palace gate;
And how the lady sate in hall,
Moaning, among her damsels all,
At the wild tale of Ronceval.
That story sounds like solemn truth,
And she would hear it with such ruth
As sympathetic hearts will pay
To moving griefs of yesterday.

Pity looked lovely in the maiden;
Her eyes were softer when so laden
With the bright dew of tears unshed.
But I was somewhat envious
That other bards should move her thus,
And oft within myself had said,

" Yea—I will strive to touch her heart
With some fair songs of mine own art."
And, many days before the day
Whereof I speak, I made assay
At this bold labour.   In the wells
Of Froissart's life-like chronicles,
I dipped for moving truths of old.
A thousand stories, soft and bold,
Of stately dames, and gentlemen,
Which good Lord Berners, with a pen
Pompous in its simplicity,
Yet tipt with charming courtesy,
Had put in English words, I learned ;
And some of these I deftly turned
Into the forms of minstrel verse.
I know the good tales are the worse—
But, sooth to say, it seems to me
My verse has sense and melody—
Even that its measure sometimes flows
With the brave pomp of that old prose.

Beneath our trysting tree, that day,
With dubious face, I read one lay.

Young Emily quite understood
My fears, and gave me guerdon good
In well-timed praise, and cheered me on
Into full flow of heart and tone.
And when, in days of pleasant weather,
Thereafter, we were met together—
As our strong love oft made us meet—
I always took my cosy seat
Just at the damsel's little feet,
And read my tales.   It was no friend
To me, that day that heard their end.
It had become a play of love
To watch the swift expression rove
Over the bright sky of her face,
To steal those upward looks, and trace
In every change of cheek and eye
The influence of my poesy.

I made my verse for Emily :
I give it, reader, now to thee.
The tales, which I have toiled to tell,
Of dame in hall, and knight in selle,

Of faithful love, and courage high—
Bright flower, strong staff of chivalry—
These tales, indeed, are old of date,
But why should Time their force abate?
Must we look back with vision dull
On the old brave and beautiful—
All careless of their joy or wo,
Because they lived so long ago?
If sympathy knows but to-day,
If time quite wears its nerve away—
If deeds majestically bold,
In words of ancient music told,
Are only food for studious minds,
And touch no hearts—if man but finds
An abstract virtue in the faith
Which clung to truth, and courted death—
If he can lift the dusky pall
With dainty hand artistical,
And smile at woes, because some years
Have swept between them and his tears—
I say, my friend, if this may be,
Then burn old books; antiquity

Is no more than a skeleton
Of painted vein, and polished bone.

Reader ! the minstrel brotherhood,
Earnest to soothe thy listening mood,
Were wont to style thee *gentle*, *good*,
Noble or *gracious* :—they could bow
With loyal knee, yet open brow—
They knew to temper thy decision
With graces of a proud submission.
That wont is changed.   Yet I, a man
Of this new land republican,
Where insolence wins upward better
Than courtesy—that old dead letter—
And toil claims pay, with utterance sharp,
Follow the good lords of the harp,
And dub thee with each courtly phrase—
And ask indulgence for my lays.

FROISSART BALLADS.

THE MASTER OF BOLTON.

PART I.

Young Gawen, from his castle wall,
Has heard the merry mavis call;
But Gawen better loves to hark
The warble of the morning lark.
That better bird is up to meet
The sun, with music proud and sweet.
A wonder is the song he sings—
And like the notes of charmed strings.
Just now his lay was all of earth,
Of sorrow intertoned with mirth,
But now, triumphant in his steven,
He mounts him to the ruddy heaven—
Making all humbler singers dumb
With his divine delirium.

3 *

Young Gawen views the fallow deer
Peopling the wide park far and near.
Some browse beneath the dewy shades,
Which edge the sunlight of the glades;
And some stare forth with earnest eyes
To greet a wandering hart whose cries
Break on the wild bird's melodies.

Kind nature, with a lavish hand,
Had poured her beauties on that land;
But Gawen, from his castle wall,
Looked moodily upon them all.
For he was born of gentle sires,
And in his bosom burned their fires,
And much it chafed his pride, to be
Shut from the pale of his degree,
By the base wants of poverty.
His sires, the knights of Bolton, were
Masters of spreading lands and fair.
Their lordly hold is stately still
On the green beauty of its hill;

But servitors, with busy din,
Break not the desert gloom within.
And over walls and portal towers
The ivy tod is weaving bowers.

A hundred steeds once fed in stall :
One freckled gray is left of all—
And he is stiff of joint and lean.
Once he was swift, and strong, and keen
As ever bore knight in harnasine.
White Raoull is his stately name,
And from a foreign land he came.
The master's sire, by dint of sword,
Won the brave steed at Castle Nord
From Raoull de Coucy, a Frankish lord.

Whilst Gawen mused in sombre cheer,
A noise of hoofs came on his ear ;
And soon a goodly company
Over the lea came ambling by—
A horseman and two ladies gay.
Flaunting and brave was their array,
And they rode talking by the way.

The master, as the three drew on
Soon knew his neighbour stout Sir John,
And, in the flaunting ladies twain
His daughters Mistress Meg, and Jean.
A London knight was sleek Sir John
Who, lending gold, took lands in pawn.
The masters of Bolton had sometime made
Acquaintance with this knight of trade—
The dismal end need scarce be said.
The Boltons of Bolton have had their day ;
Their wide fair lands have passed away.
Park, and meadow, and wood and lea—
As far as the circling hawk can see—
Sir John hath gotten them in fee.
Ah ! Master Gawen brooks it ill,
That brave new mansion on the hill !

Ruddy Sir John, with jingling rein,
Ambled between his daughters twain ;
Three spotted spaniels ran before ;
Each damsel on her round wrist bore
A jessèd and hooded sparrowhawk.
I say they cheered their way with talk,

And it rose clearly, from the bent,
Up to the master, where he leant
Over the frowning battlement.

Quoth Meg, " As proud as he may be,
The master's hall looks beggarly."
Quoth stout Sir John, " I prithee, dear,
Bridle thy tongue—the youth may hear."
But upspake Jean, the gentler maid,
And, scanning the grim pile, boldly said,
" Now, by my troth, were I as he,
A brave man lost in poverty,
The world a better tale should tell;
For I would vault into my selle
And shake my reins in proud farewell,
And bear my fortune on my lance
Over the narrow sea to France.
And where brave deeds were to be done
And lordly honours to be won,
Thither would I all odds to brave.
Better to win a gallant grave
Than cower to fortune like a slave."

The master turned him from the wall,
   Nor hearkened farther word.
He mused, and said, " I live in thrall,
   But I have freedom heard."
And more he. said, with kindling eyes,
" The burgher's little maid is wise !
Yea, I will take my sword and lance,
And ride into the realm of France,
And find in arms what meed I can,
For I am but a landless man.
In France my father won high fame,
And honour, to the Bolton name ;
And even for his gallant sake,
As well as my good way to make,
Will I this journey undertake."

And when the news went up and down
That Gawen for the field was boune,
Ten varlets, and a little page,
Out of good love, and not for wage,
Gathered to Bolton speedily,
To ride with him beyond the sea.

The varlets were stalwart Kentishmen,
The page was Philip Hazelden—
A merry boy, with boyish skill
To rob hard fortune of its ill.
The boy had been a lady's page,
But that chain galled his riper age—
Such life seemed passing dull and tame,
And so the truant fled his dame,
And valiantly to Bolton came,
In velvet hose, and jerkin trim,
And gallant on a palfrey slim
Craving, for simple boon, that he
The valiant master's page might be.

Thirty leagues below Calais,
The Master of Bolton held his way,
Mounted upon his grim old gray.
White Raoull snuffed the wind that fanned
His stately crest—he knew that land.
The pleasant touch of his native ground
Quickened his hoofs to bold rebound.
Too proud for capricole or neigh,
He yet went snorting by the way.

And, comrade from the Kentish shore,
A tercel* hawk the master bore :
A gallant bird, but now of mood
Chafed by the darkness of his hood.

The master looked with thoughtful eye
Out on the fields of Picardy.
It was the time when autumn yields
Her riches from the browning fields—
What time the vineyard on the hill
Blushes the purple press to fill ;
But bare were the lands of Picardy,
For there had been the Jacquerie,
With the wild curse of sword and fire.
The corn lay trampled in the mire,
The vineyards—pale and vine—were down,
And ruin lay on tower and town.
How sad to see those lovely lands
Made desolate by native hands !

---

* Tercel or Tercelet,—the male falcon. The female was gene-
rally used in hawking, being larger and of brighter plumage.

As Gawen rode in stately wise,
The sunlight faded in the skies ;
But wilder lights began to spread
Up to the blue vault overhead—
The baleful lights of dread Bon Home.
So rode he downward from the Somme,
With none to check his valiant will.
But five leagues south of Abbeville,
Climbing a sudden ridge, he heard
Sounds terrible, and wild, and weird,
Upswelling from the farther plain.
He checked his course with instant rein ;
And then he said, "Their howls begin :
These dread sounds are the mighty din
Of Laonois and Beauvosin.
The devils are loose ; but let us ride
A little up this good hill side."

They reached the top and thence looked down.
Beneath them lay a burning town ;
Spreading suburbs, and girdling wall—
The raging flames were over all.

4

Only by fits the wind broke through
And bared the town's red heart to view—
Showing the glare of roof and spire,
Through shifting lanes walled high with fire.
And strangely muffled by the flame,
Wailing upon the south wind came,
With alternating fall and swell,
The wild alarum of a bell.
The shades of night were darkling down,
But that red day still lit the town,
And shed its lustres, luridly,
Outward upon the heaving sea
Of the far crowding Jacquerie.

The master turned him from the sight,
And saw a castle on his right;
Westward, a league away, it stood
Rising above an autumn wood.
The forest shades lay dark, and deep,
At base of grisly tower, and keep,
But, glistering in the upper air,
Some turrets caught the ghastly glare.

The master looked forth earnestly,
And, " Comrades, we must make, " quoth he,
" Yon castle strong our hostelrie."
He stayed no farther word to say,
But rode upon the westward way.

Downward he passed at gentle speed,
And came upon a little mead—
A meadow of the freshest green,
Its verdure bright with a dewy sheen,
For there no curse of strife had been—
And crossed the waters of a rill :
But ere he climbed the opposing hill,
His way again found check, for he
Heard in the gloaming suddenly
The sounding strokes of a courser's feet,
And then was ware of a horseman fleet
Coming his slower course to meet.
He checked his steed, and poised his lance
Awaiting the horseman's swift advance.
The coming, so heard, could not be seen,
For the broad hill that rose between ;

But soon the rider drew in sight,
And Gawen saw, in the waning light,
A lithe young page on a palfrey white.
He rode on the way with turning head,
And body advanced, as one who fled
Ghastly, and white, and all adread;
Nor did he seem the band to see
As he came on so desperately.
And when as Gawen bade him stand,
The rein had well-nigh left his hand.
But when he marked the cavalier
And the mailed men-at-arms, his fear
Gave sudden way to bolder cheer.

Question abrupt brought quick reply;
The page recounted speedily
The story of his eager race.
He told the tale with reddening face;
How a right noble company,
Lords and ladies of high degree,
Riding in strength for Brennesville,
Were hard beset beyond the hill—

The lords of Roos, and Monthelesme,
And other lords of knightly fame,
And many a damosell, and dame,
Lovely ladies of noble name,
Beset in desperate case, pardie,
By a wild band of Jacquerie.
Quoth the young page, " I held aloof,
Then saved myself by speed of hoof."
" Craven !" said little Hazelden,
" The cause of dames should make us men"—
But the bold master checked his say,
And turned the strange page on his way :
Saying to all, " Good comrades, ride !
For, let all evil chance betide,
Foul breach it were of honour's laws
To strike no blow in such a cause."
With these bold words he took the lead,
And urged White Raoull to his speed.

So Gawen, with his following,
Drew on to where, in stubborn ring,

Fencing their dames as best they might,
The knights of France waged desperate fight.
He saw not, by the doubtful light,
How the ring held, but he might mark
The foe in masses dense and dark
Beating its iron fence amain.
Short space the daring youth drew rein;
Swiftly he ordered his merry men,
And placed in the midst young Hazelden,
(The stranger page had flown agen);
Then signing the cross upon his brow,
And saying, " St. George ride with me now !"
He struck the sharp spurs rowel-deep,
And, with a cry, charged down the steep.

The dark crowd swayed disorderly
Even from the master's battle cry,
And ere a lance bore stain of blood,
The nearer edge gave back a rood,
Confusedly pressing man on man ;
But when the deadly work began—

When full in their midst the swift charge burst,
When lances ravened with fiery thirst,
When stroke of sword, and plunge of horse,
Bore their hardiest down perforce,
The whole dense mass gave way outright,
And covered the wold in howling flight.
Stout Gawen rode on their rear apace—
The Frankish knights joined in the chace;
The moon, so ghastly in the air,
The wide sky's universal glare
Lighted the rout, and clown on clown
Beneath the avenging hands went down:
To say the truth, for many a rood,
A steam went up from the shedden blood.
And so that noble Frankish band—
Lords and ladies of the land—
Were won from death and outrage dire,
By prowess of the wandering squire,
Young Gawen, and his merry-men bold.
As I have said, so is it told;
In the true chronicle, we read
That Gawen Bolton did that deed.

And when the bloody chace was done,
The master praise and honour won
From knightly tongues and radiant eyes;
He answered that his poor emprise
Had found most bountiful reward—·
It was a man's best task to guard
Dames so gentle from dire mischance.
But then he said, " My Lords of France,
In God's name bide not longer here."
This counsel found right ready ear,
And the worn troop, without delay,
Resumed its interrupted way.
Ten men-at-arms were reft of life:
A score came wounded from the strife—
With bruise of club, and stab of knife—
But these found life and strength enow,
To sit their steeds, and ride, I trow;
Only the Lord of Reyneval
Was lorn of strength, among them all,
To ride beyond those perilous bounds,
And his worst hurt was not of wounds.
Time had stricken the ancient lord
With stroke more sure than stroke of sword.

But cloaked, from hoary head to spur,
In fur of stoat, and miniver,
And propped by grooms upon his horse,
The old man dared the darksome course.
Some space beyond the field of blood,
Rose the fair castle of the wood,
Whose towers had caught the master's eye;
But now the urgent train swept by,
And, crossing the line of Normandy,
Reached Brennesville, in weary plight,
After the middle watch of night.

PART II.

It boots not here, at length to tell,
In full terms of the chronicle,
How lords and dames, of high degree,
Used all fair arts of courtesy,
To win the master to their will,
And stay his course in Brennesville:
How he gainsaid them, and would fain
Have journeyed into Aquitaine:

But how high revels bred delay,
And held him from his southward way.
In the true chronicle we learn
That the great lords made fair return
For the brave stranger's timely aid—
Such fair return as might be made
By puissant lords, of fame and worth,
To a poor squire of gentle birth.
The bounteous lord of Monthelesme—
Himself of high chivalric fame—
Gave from his stalls a sable steed,
Renowned for courage, strength, and speed.
Strong was Inguerrant of body and limb,
The toils of war were a joy to him;
The valleys of Auvergne bred his sire,
But Besarabia gave him fire,
For he was born of a Servian dam.
A thousand florins of the Lamb
The good Lord Roos gave graciously—
A gift of love and not a fee—
And five full purses, of the ten,
The master lavished to his men.

But the old Lord of Reyneval,
The sooth to say, surpassed them all.
He gave a suit of knightly mail,
Tempered to hue of silver pale,
Inlaid with arabesques of gold,
And cunning traceries manifold—
All made by a famous artisan
Edmè Paol of fair Milan :—
Adding, with courteous intent,
Some wealth of peaceful ornament,
A loop of pearls and turquoise band.
These gave he by his ward's white hand ;
His ward, the Countess Jocelind,
Heiress of stately Rousillon,
Deigned in her courtesy to bind
The pearl-loop to his morion,
And clasped the band upon his throat.
Her fine fair fingers thrilled, I wot,
And the bold master said, " It were
A thing of less than naught to dare
Perils of earth, and sea, and air,
For a love touch from hands so white,
For a love look from eyes so bright."

The gifts, I know, were rare and proud,
But the good lords and knights avowed
To all who heard their words, that he,
By prowess of unbought chivalry,
Had rescued them from certain death
In harness on that bloody heath,
And high-born damosell and dame
From tortures of a hellish shame.

And then it chanced that, day by day,
The valiant master made delay,
From trial of his southward way;
Shunning all thought of fair Guienne—
Of his great Prince and countrymen—
Or, if he might not shun the thought,
Saying, " My master needs me not,
For there is present truce with France;
If the truce fail, as scarce may chance,
Then will I mount my steed agen,
And join his banner in Guienne."
But, I am bound to say the truth,
A lady's eyes enthralled the youth—

The dark blue eyes of Jocelind.
The days, like barques before the wind,
Flew swiftly by ; and as they passed
The spell grew complicate and fast.
Sweet skill of undesigned art
Fettered the strong man, limb and heart.
Sore wrestled he, and stoutly strove
For freedom from a desperate love :
But feeble eld is stronger far
To wage such shrewd and subtil war
Than youth, whose very fire and force
Plunge into toils beyond recourse.
And so the master tarried still,
A thrall of love, in Brennesville.

Meanwhile the Duke of Normandy*
Upheld his banner, by the sea,
In leaguer of St. Valery.
For troubles of intestine war—
Hot feuds of Bourbon and Navarre—

---

* Dauphin, and Regent of France—his father, King John,
being prisoner of Edward III. of England.

Were rife in France, since good King John,
His ransom merks unpaid, had gone
Back to captivity, to bear—
Worse than captivity—despair—
Uncrowned, but kingly in his truth!
His son, of Normandy, a youth
Of gallant promise, ruled his realm,
Wearing for crown a soldier's helm,
And lay, I said, beside the sea,
In leaguer of St. Valery.
Proud Monthelesme and Roos rode forth
To join his standard in the North;
But the sick Lord of Reyneval
Tarried behind in peaceful hall.

The dames, deserted of their knights,
Grew weary of the tame delights
Of courtly life, and did decree
Divertisements of falconry.
And so one autumn morn it chanced
That, in fair train, these ladies pranced,
On gallant palfreys, from a port,
To spend the day abroad in sport.

Gawen beside the countess went,
And all sweet cares and service lent.
The lady heard him, and caressed
A falcon tercel on her wrist.
His speech, I say, the lady heard,
And so, I trow, did the stately bird,
And shook his hooded head, and screamed
In recognition glad, it seemed.
"Sieur Gawen, the bird," said Jocelind,
"So darkened by the hood, is blind,
But he is full of joy to hear,
And know, his former lord so near."
It was the bird the master bore·
Over sea, from the Kentish shore.
The bird he had flown in calm and wind
On Kent's broad wealds in earlier days,
But now hath given to Jocelind :—
And she the courtesy repays,
And calls him by the master's name,
Which, sounded forth in mandate shrill,
Will ever the falcon's flight reclaim,
And bend his wild heart to her will.

The haughty bird is willing thrall,
And loves the lady's silver call.

Riding at amble, on a down,
A league beyond the trodden town,
Some object came to Gawen's ken,
And forth he called young Hazelden.
" Come hither, boy,"—the master said.
The page rode up unbonneted—
" Now ride to yonder knoll; I deem
I saw, just now, a banner gleam ;
Use well thine eyes."   The page turned rein,
And rode the distant knoll to gain.
" A comely page"—said Jocelind—
" And like mine own, whose fate unkind
I grieve.   Poor Huon ! since the night,
When thou didst find this wandering wight"—
" Forget," the modest master said,
" That peril, and my feeble aid.
But, noble lady, since the boy—
I trust he met with no annoy—

Hath scorned the lure, nor comes agen,
Take thou fair Philip Hazelden.
For his poor master's sake, and thine,
The boy, I think, will well incline
To serve thee; at his tender age,
The child should be a lady's page—
Not share the fortunes of my band."
The countess placed her gloved hand
Softly on Gawen's arm, and smiled;
Then said, " Sieur Gawen, I will take—
Thy rare and noble gift—the child,
And guard him for his master's sake.
But the boy loves such peril wild
Of camps and battle-fields, and he
May scorn my silken page to be."

Ere the good master made reply,
All heard a merry signal cry,
And a swift heron, from a marsh,
Mounted, with sudden scream, and harsh,
Beating the air in wild alarm.
Then hawks were cast from many an arm;

5*

And it was a gallant sight to see
The fleet birds tower so valiantly,
Each for the vanguard challenging.
But none went forth so swift of wing—
Mounted so boldly on the wind,
As the brave bird of Jocelind.

With winnow, and soar, he won the height,
At point above the quarry's flight,
And balanced in air, and made his stoop;
But the swift heron shunned the swoop,
And, wheeling aside, a moment stayed
Just over the gazing cavalcade;
A wild-eyed, terror-stricken bird,
The Kentish hawk had canceliered,
But now drove back upon his prey,
Ire-whetted for the fresh assay.
The lady's heart with pity filled
The quarry's mortal dread to see,
And, in her gentleness, she willed
To ward its dire extremity.
With uplift hands, and eager eyes,
And cheeks bereft of their rosy dyes—

" GAWEN, MY GAWEN, COME BACK," she cried.

The hawk, true vassal, turned aside,

Doubtful upon his pinions wide,

Then, like the servant of a charm,

Sank to his perch on the lady's arm.

The damsel, in her loveliness,

Made lovelier by that kind distress,

Repaid the bold bird's loyalty,

With gentleness of hand, and eye,

That silver call, so sweet to hear,

When will it die on the master's ear?

" My Gawen—come back !"—the truth to say,

He pondered the words for many a day.

But he must win from his dream amain,

His page rides fast to join the train.

The boy's bright visage augured well

Of stirring news, and blithe, to tell.

He stopped his course at Gawen's side;

" What have your ousel eyes espied ?"

" A gallant host," the boy replied,

" A royal army, foot and horse."

And Gawen said, " The regent's force

Is drawing from the northern sea,
As the news went, for Picardy."

And soon they mark the vanguard come
With trumpet blast, and storm of drum ;
And proudly in the midst unrolled,
Blazoned with fleurs de lis of gold,
The royal standard woos the wind.
Pennon, and pennoncelle behind,
And crest of high-born cavalier,
And sheen of burnished helm, and spear,
Along the lengthened lines appear.
The son of France rode in the van,
With many a stately gentleman
Attendant on his presence high ;
And when the fair train met his eye,
Brief pause he made, but left his post
In vanguard of the moving host,
And joined the dames, with greeting fair,
And a glad port and debonair.
Certes a gallant youth was he,
And owned chivalric fealty,
To the sweet powers of feminie.

Right pleasant were the words he spake,
And many a courtly jest he brake
With laughing damosell and dame.
And so, returning, slowly came
The host, and train, to reach the town.
The menzy saw them drawing down,
And with loud thunders rent the sky,
In welcome of their chivalry.

In the true chronicle of old,
We find the truth right fitly told,
That when the Dauphin heard aright
Of Gawen's deed, he dubbed him knight;
And that—the tale he heard so wrought
With his own valorous heart—he sought
Sir Gawen's service to engage,
At cost of lands, and annual wage.
To this, Sir Gawen, courteously,
Urged back his English fealty,
And still affirmed his purpose good—
With all fair show of gratitude—

To take horse with his Kentishmen,
And join the Black Prince in Guienne.

But whilst Sir Gawen held him still
In the proud court of Brennesville,
He found a limner great of skill,
And bought his art, with golden fee,
To paint a scene of falconry.
The limner painted Jocelind,
And that fleet falcon on the wind.
The lady's hands have lost the rein,
Which lies upon her jennet's mane,
And are uplifted whitherward
Her blue eyes fix their full regard;
Some tresses of her flaxen hair
Stream forth a little on the air;
There is no colour on her cheek,
Her quick lips seem to cry, not speak;
And the bold hawk, with downward eye,
Pauses to question of her cry.
A shining legend on a scroll
Beneath, gave meaning to the whole.

" Gawen, my Gawen, come back !"—such were
The golden words of the legend fair.

Ere Gawen went on pilgrimage,
He gave the picture, and his page,
To the sweet lady of his love.
And, fair return, her broidered glove
He wore upon his basnet bright.
The proudest dame may choose her knight—
Bold champion of her scarf or glove—
Yet deign no tender thought of love.
So Gawen deemed, and dared not speak
The passion glowing on his cheek.
Like a Chaldean to his star,
He poured his worship from afar.

It boots not now, in terms, to say
How the boy page was loth to stay
Behind, from trial of that way.
Suffice it, when the knight took rein
For the fair realm of Aquitaine,
Young Philip rode not with his train.

Nor boots it now in terms to tell
What on that course the knight befell;
Or how Black Edward—far the while
From solace of the happy isle—
Gave to his coming gladsome cheer,
And, of his fatherland to hear,
Much used the knight's society.
My story's progress may not be
Diverted from that single end,
Whither its steps, impatient, tend.

PART III.

Attended by her happy hours,
    The maiden May walks garlanded;
The earth is beautiful with flowers,
    And birds are jocund overhead.
Wide valleys, verdant from the showers,
    By fertile cares of April shed,
Give promise, to the hungry towers,
    Of summer fruits, and autumn bread.

Look forth upon the hills, and see
   The dark-green umbrage of the vine!
This year she promises to be
   A liberal mother with her wine.
And mark the peasants on the lea,
   Dancing, in joyous intertwine
Of swift limbs, to the melody
   Of dull tambour, and viol fine.

Black Edward, and his isle-born men,
Have crowned the brows of peace agen,
And given her empery in Guienne;
To such fair land, to such sweet time,
Pass with the swift need of my rhyme.

The lists were closed at Castellon,
   And, in a palace high
Builded beside the broad Dordogne,
   That flower of chivalry—
Black Edward—sate, in careless state,
   At banquet with his knights,
Discoursing arms, and ladies' charms,
   Brave deeds, and soft delights.

6

Alone of all in banquet hall,
   Sir Gawen's troubled eyne
Denied the power of that high hour,
   Its flow of mirth and wine.
" Thou cloud upon our fellowship !"
   Such words his master said,
" What care is this upon thy lip
   To scorn the wine so red ?"
Then Gawen made this answer true,
   " Ah ! sire, some words of thine
Have lent the bitterness of rue
   Unto the ruddy wine.
Virgilius sings of one who shot
   An arrow at the sky,
And I, with like audacious thought,
   Have aimed my love too high."
Bold answer made the Prince, and laughed—
   " If she, who quells thy glance,
Sits perched too high for flight of shaft,
   Essay her with thy lance.
Virgilius was a troubadour
   Of excellent renown ;

But, nathless, brave deeds are a lure
   To win a princess down.
Take instance from another bard!
   A squire of low degree,
By prowess, won young Ermingarde,
   Princess of Hungary."

The Prince so answered and confessed
The swift wine's power: ungirded vest—
Bold cheeks empurpled by the dyes
Of jocund Bacchus—glittering eyes—
And volant speech—gave token free
Of the blithe god's supremacy.

Meantime a warder paced in state,
Clanking before the palace gate,
And humming, as he paced, a lay
Of the good island far away.
The notes were sad as sad could be,
For the brave warder Willoughby
Had looked upon the northern star
And thought him of his home afar,

His home by silver Wye's fair side;
And—softened from his warrior pride—
Of one who might have been his bride,
But for the wildness of his youth.
He sang, and sighed—and said, " Sweet Ruth !
There was a time when thou and I
Were happy on the banks of Wye;
But wayward was my youth and blind—
I broke thy gentle heart and kind.
Idle the wish, and worse than vain,
But would that day were back again !"
And tears bedimmed the warder's sight,
As he looked far into the night,
To watch the loadstar's silver light.

Whilst the stout warder paced in state,
Wheeling before the palace gate,
And mused his exile lot aright,
A horseman shouted from the night.
The warder bade him errand show,
And stayed his own proud pace and slow,
Fitting an arrow to his bow.

But the free rider blithely spake—
" Yon red lights show a princely wake :
Say if the knight of Bolton be
At banquet with the chivalry."
" That knight is at the wassail now,"
Said Willoughby, " but who art thou ?"
Lightly the stranger left his steed—
A noble boy in way worn weed—
And pressed his suit, that he, with speed,
Might pass the gates—for that he bore
Hot errand to the knight : much more
His quick speech urged, and Willoughby
Gave to the stranger entrance free.

" Master"—a voice of slender sound
Reached Gawen's ear : he turned him round.
The low sweet voice he heard agen.
It was fair Philip Hazelden.
And now he stands, with beaming eyes,
Silent before·the knight's surprise.
Amidst the flow of wine, it seemed
To good Sir Gawen that he dreamed.

6*

But this soon passed, and in his joy
The knight embraced the gentle boy.
" Dear child," he said, " show now to me
Why thou art come from Normandy."
And Philip gave into his hands,
A casket small with burnished bands.
A touch soon drew the bands asunder,
And then Sir Gawen saw, with wonder,
The picture, which the limner's skill
Had whilome made in Brennesville.
He marks the Lady Jocelind—
Her pity-beaming eyes—her hair
A little streaming on the air:
He marks the falcon on the wind—
Then letters of that legend fair :
" GAWEN—MY GAWEN—COME BACK !"—I trow
The words have flushed Sir Gawen's brow.
He marks them clearly by the gleam
Of the brave torches : doth he dream ?
Doth that proud lady of the land
Utter to *him* the sweet command

To come again ?   Her messenger
Perchance may prove interpreter.
He turned him swiftly to the youth.
" Dear boy," he said, " say out the truth."
And the page said with earnest tone,
Which reached Sir Gawen's ear alone,
" My lady lies in grievous wo,
And, in her sorrow, bids me show
To brave Sir Gawen that her fate
Will poorly brook his coming late.
The dying Lord of Reyneval
Is vowed to hold a tourney high,

   Open to all
   True chivalry

Of England, Alemaigne, and France ;
And, guerdon to the winning lance
In combat waged at utterance,
He firmly saith his ward shall be.
For he is in extremity
Of feeble age, and France is torn

   By discord dire ;

He will not leave the damsel lorn,
   And meet her sire
Beyond the gates of death, which now
Ope for him, with a broken vow
   Vile on his soul;
And so fair field he will allow
   And free control
Of the good laws of chivalry;
And he who doth most valiantly,
Shall win the maid, and wide fair lands,
And he will gild the nuptial bands
With added wealth—for love, not hate,
Hath urged such course his ward to mate.

 " And the sad lady bids me say,
In such fair phrases as I may,
That, if she errs not of thy love,
And thou wouldst win the hand whose glove
Is on thy basnet, thou must haste.
Something she said of maiden chaste
Constrained by fate such words to speak;
And blushes deepened on her cheek;

She knew not what thyself might deem,
And feared such course would ill beseem
A maiden in her purity :
But her true heart, and destiny,
Bade her forget observance fine
And rest her feeble hand in thine."

A red light streamed from Gawen's eyes,
His visage burned with sanguine dyes.
Himself, to hark, he did command,
But crushed a goblet in his hand.
And, when the tale was said, the boy
He seized, and wrought him sore annoy
With fury of his glad embrace.
" Now, by our blessed Lady's grace !"
He cried, " the tale thou tellest, child,
Hath reft my sense, and made me wild.
Thou art a herald brighter far
Than the blithe morning's vaward star,
And well hast driven my gloom away
With golden promise of the day."
" My Prince !"—he bowed at Edward's knee —
" My Prince, I crave a boon of thee.

I read not with my glooming eye
The omen of thy counsel high,
But now may read; it well may chance
That I, even I, with humble lance,
Wreathed by no splendours of renown,
 Shall win my lofty lady down."

The board was hushed, and Gawen told
The truth, with joyous lip and bold,
To the brave Prince, and knights in hall—
How the good Lord of Reyneval
Was vowed to hold a tourney high,
Free to the gentle chivalry
Of England, Alemaigne, and France;
And guerdon to the winning lance,
In combat waged at utterance,
Would yield—he paused ere more he said,
And his brow darkened from its red:
But he spake on—" For guerdon good,
Prize to the stoutest man at arms—
Perchance some soldier, stern and rude—
That lord will yield the maid, whose charms

Are my soul's star.   Grant, sire, that I
May ride to win that prize, or die."

The Prince unclasped his ruff's fine band,
Then leant his cheek upon his hand,
And read Sir Gawen with an eye
Wise with the wine's solemnity.
" I doubt," he said, " if knightly *laws*
Should gild success in such a cause.
A bugle horn may fitly be
Prize in a game of archerie;
A runlet, and a Lincoln gown
Guerdon the strife of clown with clown.
But, by St. George! it seems not well
That a true-hearted damosell,
In modesty of maidenhood,
Should bide the fate of jousting rude.
When the first Romans won that course
In tourney with the Sabine horse,
Each knight, for guerdon of his game,
Seized to himself a Sabine dame.

But this, sir knight, the clerks agree,
Covered the Roman chivalry
With the world's scorn and infamy.
I know it is the wont of France
To hang such issues on the lance,
Also of lands beyond the Rhine—
That river of the sapient vine ;
But nathless, in our better land,
We win not so a lady's hand.
Seeking the hand, we wile the heart
With strategies of manly art.
Besides, such wooing of the sword
Binds shrewish mate to wretched lord."

He ceased: Sir Gawen spake more low,
And the full truth essayed to show.
Black Edward heard him, and replied—
" If thou may'st win a willing bride,
Get thee to horse, good knight and tried ;
And, certes, of these gentlemen,

  A band will ride,
To prove the prowess of Guienne
  By Seine's fair side.

The friend of Edward should not be
A needy child of errantry,
And leave his court, to journey forth
Like a Scots horseman of the north.
Strife for the maid of Rousillon—
Sir Gawen's mistress—be his own.
The knights of France—none worthier live
In any land—will doubtless give
To all, such entertainment good
Of arms, and feats of hardihood,
As well may stay the sturdiest mood.
By my own knighthood! I would fain
Myself join stout Sir Gawen's train,
And leave my cares of Aquitaine
To hark the bugles of the Seine."
And the brave knights, with blithe accord,
Welcomed the fair speech of their lord,
With thunders of the banquet board.

Felton, La Poule, and Percy bold—
So is the old true story told—

With other knights of good renown,
By the next midday left the town.
Sir Gawen went upon the way,
Mounted upon his stately gray.
The sable steed, with haughty tread,
Came after, by a stout groom led :—
A charger worthy to uphold
A monarch, when his crown of gold
Totters upon his royal brows,
And he arrays, with muttered vows,
The broken remnants of his host
From turmoil of a battle lost,
To dare, in storm of final strife,
Issues of empire, death, and life.

So journeying earnestly, the band
Drew freely to the northern land ;
And by the way, brave rumours heard—
For the wide country side was stirred—
Of open lists, and knightly sport,
In presence of the Regent's court,
At the good town of Bar-by-Seine.
The earnest horsemen rode amain—

Their swift desire brooked small delay—
And soon drew on to Fontenay.
There heard they certain news at last
That three days of the jousts were past;
That Eustace, Lord of Saimpi, held
Possession of the listed field.
That lord had done his devoir well;
Himself scarce shaken in his selle,
His lance nine knights had overthrown—
To bide his mighty brunt was none.
And, with the news, came doubtful tale
Of sorrows of the maiden pale,
Young Jocelind of Rousillon,
For whose fair hand such course was run.
For five days were the jousts decreed,
Three days were past, and urgent need
Was now to press their way with speed.

Past Cravant, riding in the land
Of fair Champaign, the English band,
Worn by the route, made brief delay
At a good hostel by the way.

Biding to mend their travel's want,
The knights sent on a pursuivant,
To Charles, the Regent, to declare
Their near approach, and purpose fair.

The lists were ordered, on a plain,
A little north of Bar-by-Seine,
And now, what time the band delay
At the good hostel by the way,
The barriers of the lists are down,
And Charles comes riding from the town.
.Hark to the trumpet's shrill fanfare,
And the glad shouts that rend the air!
The sun is at his midday height,
But fleecy clouds half veil his light;
And breathing freshly of the main,
A far-flown wind sighs up the Seine.
So the glad riders all will say
Some words in honour of the day,
As marshalled onward by the din
They pass, in state, the lists to win.

The Regent on his hackney goes,
Crowned with a chaplet of the rose.
Such sportive wreath suits better far
Than crown of state, or helm of war
With the soft beauty of his brow.
And all who mark him will avow
That fate ne'er bound the weightier care
Of a realm's rule on locks so fair.
And stern men note his girlish bloom,
Mating so well with rose and plume,
And, softened from their sternness, say
" Now let him win, whenas he may,
Pastime in sportive holiday,
And his proud ringol put away.
Our royal boy is wise with youth,
And well eludes the colder truth—
Cheating his cares, which are his foes,
With sweet deceptions of the rose."

So passing on his hackney stout,
Charles•led the vanguard of the rout,
And reached the lists ; then left his steed,
With a right gallant grace, to lead

The white-browed maid of Rousillon,
Queen of the tourney, to her throne.
Pale as a white flower is her cheek—
Pale and without one ruddy streak ;
Her eyes are sad, but stern and proud—
Sad with a sorrow unavowed—
Stern with a strength of heart unbowed.
From her sweet lips, of late so bright,
Gone are the roses of delight.
The subtil tide which late distained
Their ripeness, wearying cares have drained,
And their wan lines are much compressed
With stern resolve and wild unrest.
Pray God the damsel's dark-blue eyes
May sparkle soon in happier wise,
And cheek and lip win back their dyes.

PART IV.

Before his tent Lord Saimpi stood,
    And scornfully did say—
" Small hope is there, by holy rood !
    Of knightly sport to-day.

Will none of all take heart of grace
　　To meet my swift career?
This countess, sure, is dark of face,
　　Or I have bred a fear.
Go, page, and bid my bugler sound
　　A blast upon his horn."
He cast a jeering look around—
　　He spake the words in scorn.

Of willing knights, who heard, I trow,
　　There was not any want,
And many a scowl, and bended brow
　　Answered Lord Saimpi's vaunt.
Much burned the lusty bachelours
　　The boastful knight to tame;
But they were bound by their amours,
　　And might not dare the game.
Upspake the Regent—" Is there none
　　The course will undertake,
And meet this doughty champion
　　For the sweet lady's sake?"

Even as he spoke, a winded horn
   Rang out with sudden sound,
And a stout courier, travel-worn,
   Entered the listed ground.

" Now, courier, say whence comest thou—
   What errand dost thou bear ?"
Answer he made with covered brow,
   Nor deigned he preface fair.
Much lacked the wight of courtesy,
   He cast no word away,
But, upright in his saddle tree,
   Right stoutly said his say.
" Lord Arundel, Sir John Cathore,
   Of England, Sieur Herchaunce
Of Rhineland, from the northern shore
   Draw on to break a lance—
If France so will it—in the game
   For a fair lady's hand,
Whereof advertisement of fame
   Hath reached the northern land."

" Now, Lord of Clary ! speed thee well—
 Ride with a gallant train,
And greet the good Lord Arundel,
 And greet his comrades twain.
Fail nothing of our state, pardie—
 Stint nothing of their due ;
In honours of a welcome free
 Be thou our vicar true."
Even as he spoke, a winded horn
 Rang out with sudden sound :
Again a horseman, travel-worn,
 Entered the listed ground.

" Now, horseman, say whence comest thou—
 What errand dost thou bear ?"
Answered the wight with reverent brow,
 And after preface fair—
" My masters, gallant gentlemen
 Of the Duke Edward's court,
Have journeyed hither from Guienne
 For share of knightly sport.

The knights of Felton, Parthenay,
   La Poule, and Percy tried,
Sir Godfrey Hall, Sir Walter Grey,
   Have deigned, for love, to ride—
Hopeful of enterprise—in train
   Of a most worthy knight,
Young, but of note in Aquitaine,
   Sir Gawen Bolton hight.
The gentle knights now make delay
At a near hamlet by the way,
And bade me ride thus much to say."

Quoth Charles, " This purse of ruddy gold
Take thou, for fair news fairly told.
Felton, La Poule, and Parthenay,
Percy, stout Hall, and Walter Grey,
Renown hath loudly bruited them !
But Edward hath no goodlier gem,
In the bright ring of valour, which
Engirds his state with lustre rich,
Than Gawen Bolton, trusty knight.
We read the gentleman aright

Some months agone ; good fortune made
His prowess instrument of aid
To many here, who now will show
Their love in grateful overflow.
Brave Lord of Clisson ! make array,
And go thou forth upon the way
With a proud train of gentlemen,
To meet the worthies of Guienne.
And bear in mind, right trusty lord—
What Christian lands, with fair accord,
Avow unquestioned truth to be—
That the sweet virtue courtesy
Hath chosen our Frankish hearts for bowers,
Wherein to rear her loveliest flowers."

I ween the maid of Rousillon—
Bending, to listen, from her throne—
Heard, with a flutter of the heart,
The messenger his tale impart,
Sir Gawen's name wrought like a spell
The maiden's dire despair to quell.

To God in heaven, with upward gaze,
And aspect beaming with the rays
Of a sweet trembling hope, she prays,
As one late rescued from despair,
And heart-assured of granted prayer.
If her fair thought had utterance won
Thus would its hopeful speech have run—
" Sir Gawen's heart is true and bold,
And, cased in armour manifold,
Of a good cause, can take no harm ;
And stalwart is the knight of arm,
Sturdy in brunt of man and horse,
And skill'd to run chivalric course.
Love, kind to all who love—the right,
Dear to high heaven—his own proud might,
These to my heart, so beating, bear
Assurance strong of issue fair."

And ere the lady's courage fell
From the high tone it held so well,
The gentlemen of Aquitaine
Appeared in distance on the plain.

The knights had taken respite brief—
For dalliance wrought Sir Gawen grief—
And, mounting, came so close behind
Their messenger, that as the wind
Shifted to meet them, they might hear
The hoof-strokes of his swift career.

Under proud escort of a band,
The noblest of the Frankish land,
The knights of merry England came.
Welcome of lord and smile of dame,
And flying tongues subdued of tone,
As the proud men-at-arms drew on,
Greeted their presence graciously.
In van of all, great Normandy
Expended many a phrase of love,
The fulness of his joy to prove.
At stately height among the rest,
His mistress saw Sir Gawen's crest,
And caught the triumph of his eye,
And read the silent speech, whereby

8

He spake his gallant hope and love.

She saw, and read the truth, and strove

Dominion of her mood to gain ;

But the sweet lady strove in vain.

Her utmost art might not repress

Tears of a hopeful happiness.

Love, in a gentle nature, rears

His home beside the fount of tears,

And scouts the art which fain would quell

The sweet flow of the crystal well.

The English cavaliers were spent

With the way's toil, and Charles, intent

To do them pleasure, did adjourn

All feats of arms until the morn.

But for my lengthened lay, I fain

Would say how sped in Bar-by-Seine

A night of revel ; how the day

Broke timeless in on banquet gay ;

How Arundel—who reached the town

An hour before the sun went down,

With John Cathore, and stout Herchaunce,—

Surpassed the gayest wits of France,

And, solemnly installed high-priest
Of the blithe wine-god, ruled the feast
Until the lighting of the east.
Sir Gawen feasted not that night,
But husbanded his force aright.
At dawn, ere yet the festive mirth
Had found an end, he sallied forth,
Saw that his steeds were brave of trim,
Healthful of mettle and of limb;
And then, returning, meekly made
His orisons for Mary's aid;
And, after, with observance shrewd,
His knightly arms and armour viewed,
For more to him than death and life
Rested on issue of the strife.

I know not if the earnest knight
Passed greeting with his lady bright.
But, rumour said, the Kentish page,
With sober step, and aspect sage,
Did pass, and errand seem to bear
Betwixt the knight and lady fair.

Now to fair field! with mandate loud
Heralds make order in the crowd,
And clear free space for man and steed.
The last day of the five decreed
Is climbing onward to its noon:
The knightly sports will ope full soon.
Where, orderly, the crowd divides,
Into the lists Sir Gawen rides
Manful upon his charger black;
Percy and Hall ride at his back,
And the bold three pass slowly round
The circle of the tourney ground,
Beneath the eyes of ladies gay,
Greeting and greeted by the way.
This done, Sir Gawen did desire
Stout Thomelyn of Kent, his squire,
To strike Lord Saimpi's shield in sign
Of gage accepted.   Thomelyn
Drew to the lord's pavilion,
Where, glistering bravely in the sun,
The broad shield hung: and, winning near,
Smote on its face, with point of spear.

Lord Saimpi issued forth with speed,
And donned his helm, and took his steed.

Now Gawen Bolton! fortune yield
   To love, and to the right,
The shelter of her magic shield;
   There is no sturdier knight,
In the wide realm of lovely France,
   Or any Christian land,
Than Saimpi's lord—in war of lance,
   Or battle-axe and brand.
But the stout islander, I trow,
   Has not a heart to faint;
In hope, not fear, he made his vow
   To his kind patron saint.
Once looked he to the golden sun—
   Once to his lady dear—
Then like a willing champion,
   Took ground for his career.

At signal of a bugle blast,
   Sharp and of sudden sound,

8*

The knights set forward, fiery fast,
    And met in middle ground :
Met with stern shock of man and horse,
    And din of crashing spears ;—
But neither champion won the course,
    They parted there like peers.

Again—again ! and respite none
    Will hot Lord Saimpi yield :
Swift he demands with haughty tone
    Renewal of the field.

Whereto, Sir Gawen, urged to speak,
    Answers, as haughtily,
" By God ! proud knight—I nothing seek
    So much as strife with thee."

Thus spake he, and his visor closed,
    As to his post he passed.
Again the armed men, opposed,
    Await the signal blast.

Sudden it came ! with hearts of flame,
    The champions, at the sound,
Drove each his steed to furious speed,
    And met in middle ground.

The Frankish champion struck amain—
   Struck with a force so dire
On Gawen's helmet, that his brain
   Streamed with a flood of fire.
But Gawen smote the knight of France
   Full on his sturdy breast,
And, driven perforce, the trusty lance
   Through shield and corslet prest—
Crashing through steel, the weapon good
   Lord Saimpi's bosom found,
Nor broke until the sudden blood
   Gushed darkly from the wound.
Manful against the lance's force
   Lord Saimpi bore him well,
And passed Sir Gawen in the course,
   All upright in his selle:
But, with the gallop of his horse,
   He reeled—and swayed—and fell.

" Now yield thee, Lord of Saimpi, yield!"
   No word Lord Saimpi said;
The fount of haughty speech was sealed,
   Lord Saimpi's life was sped—

Sped gallantly : and on his shield,
   Distained so bloody red,
His servants bore him from the field,
   At slow and solemn tread.

With the lord's death, a hush of awe
   Fell down on tongue and heart,
And you might mark the nobles draw
   In sombre groups apart.
Few were who loved the haughty lord,
And vauntful port and jeering word
   Prefaced the stroke of doom ;
But none reck now of these—the proud
Beauty, and valour, of the crowd,
   One aspect wear of gloom.
Said gentle Charles, " A woful end !
May Jesu's potent love befriend
The brave Lord Saimpi in his want.
   A rude audacity defaced—
Audacity and sins of vaunt—
   His prowess, but the knight was graced

With gallant virtues.   Better lance—
Despite that taint of arrogance—
Or stouter heart, was not in France.
Sir Gawen Bolton—all will say—
Hath borne him gallantly to-day,
And we, as right is, willingly,
Perforce of our fair powers, decree
That—Saimpi dead—this champion bold,
And proved of valiant worth, shall hold
Possession of the knightly ring,
All armed comers challenging.
All rights of field by Saimpi won,
Transferred by Saimpi, now undone,
Rest with his victor.   Cheerfully,
So much of course we now decree.
And, gallants! hearken what we say—
Who holds this field at set of day
Will bear the game's fair prize away."

Into the lists Lord Arundel—
A gay, glad knight, known passing well
In courts of kings, and famed for skill
To vanquish woman to his will,

And trained in all accomplishments
Of dance, and song, and martial fence,
And master too of dexterous art
With the sweet harp to reach the heart—
This worthy gentleman, I say,
Entered the lists with bearing gay,
And said: "For the fair lady's sake,
I humbly crave a spear to break,
When the good knight of Bolton's force
Is mended from his double course."
Whereto Sir Gawen answer made,
Gallant and fair, and nothing stayed,
But, with high heart of hopeful cheer,
And proud glance to his lady dear,
Took post again, and couched his spear.

PART V.

At signal of a bugle blast,
    Sharp and of sudden sound,
The knights set forward, fiery fast,
    And met in middle ground.

Lord Arundel struck Gawen's shield,
 And broke his spear in three—
Struck with such force that Gawen reeled
 Wild in his saddle-tree.

But Gawen smote Lord Arundel
 Full on his helmet's front,
And bowed him to his horse's tail,
 So mighty was the brunt.

And when the lord firm posture won,
 And from the shock upreared
His comely brow—his helm was gone,
 And bloody was his beard.

"Small thanks, Sir Gawen, for thy stroke"—
 Right merrily said the Lord—
"And, ere a second I provoke,
 I crave one gentle word
Of the fair Lady Jocelind,
 For whose white hand we ride.
I care not with a doubting mind
 This battle to abide."

Then passing, frank of courtesy,
 He came before the maid,

And, gallantly, from bended knee,
  In pleasant accents said,
" Sweet majesty ! an humble knight,
  Led on by brave report
Of splendours of thy beauty bright,
  I sought this Frankish court.
The real beauty, whereof fame
  So spake, outshines as far
Her best report, as Dian's flame
  Outshines a twinkling star.
Now speak a frank fair truth, and say,
  If playing well my part,
I win success, wilt thou repay
  My toil with willing heart ?"

" Sir knight," said Jocelind, " thy words
  Are gently toned, but ill.
The prouder strength of man accords
  Naught to a maiden's will.
But, for frank answer, elsewhere seek ;
  Thy skill of lance and lute
May surely win a brighter cheek,
  To redden to thy suit."

Uprose the lord : " Then will I ride
    No more to-day," quoth he,
" Lord Saimpi's fate—unwilling bride,
    Neither seems good to me."
And so the gentleman passed forth,
    And put his helm away,
And better pastime found in mirth,
    And converse light and gay.
Meantime, this controversy done,
    Sir Gawen, nothing loth,
Passed to a fair pavilion
    Of silk and samite cloth ;
And doffed his casque, and rested there,
    Whereof was earnest need,
Whilst his swift grooms, with willing care,
    Recruited well his steed.

Now who is he, so haught of head,
    Who enters on the field—
Curbs his white steed to stately tread,
    And smites Sir Gawen's shield ?

9

All marked the giant, as he passed
   At slow and stern advance,
All marked his charger strong and vast—
   All knew the knight Herchaunce.
The growing hope of Jocelind
   Before his coming bends,
And, like a taper in the wind,
   For feeble life contends.
How may her chosen knight endure
   The more than human force
Of such a foe—how hold before
   Such giant man and horse?
With beating heart, fixed eye, and cheek
   As very marble pale—
She sits, too wild of thought to seek
   Concealment of her veil.
But from his tent, Sir Gawen steps
   With gallant countenance,
And cheerfully to saddle leaps,
   And grasps his trusty lance.
At signal of a bugle blast,
   Sharp and of sudden sound,

The knights set forward, fiery fast,
 And met in middle ground.
Herchaunce, who ran the course as he
 His foe would overwhelm,
At meeting did unskilfully,
 And missed Sir Gawen's helm.
Sir Gawen struck the Rhenish knight,
 A stroke of truest force,
And bore him from his seat, outright,
 And hurled him from his horse.
Sir Gawen sprang from saddle-tree,
 And drew his dagger bright;
" Now yield, Sir Knight, or die," quoth he.
 " I yield me," said the knight.

What time this goodly end befell,
 A wondrous scene and rare—
So read we in the chronicle—
 Was clearly witnessed there.
From mastery of his rider freed,
 Inguerrant onset made
Against Herchaunce's Rhenish steed,
 Who met him naught afraid.

With clamping teeth, and nostrils wide,
    And crests right proud to see,
Rearing, and striking, in their pride,
    The steeds fought wrathfully.
Their yellow mail—their glossy skins
    Sable and snowy white,
Gleamed grandly, as the Paladins
    So waged their wondrous fight.
Before the crowding grooms might staunch
    The fury of their feud,
Both steeds, from quivering crest to haunch,
    I ween, were crimson-hued.
The Black, sore wounded, may not bear
    His master more to-day ;
And Gawen bids his grooms prepare,
    And bard, his English gray.

The long day wanes—short time remains
    Ere falling of the night—
Sir Gawen bold, if fortune hold,
    Will win his lady bright.
One champion more—Sir John Cathore—
    The combat will assay :

If evil chance weigh on *his* lance,
    Sir Gawen wins the day.
Of gentle birth, this John Cathore
    Was but a chevalier
Who sought his wage on every shore,
    And won gold with his spear.
The knight had lost his dexter eye,
    By flight of shaft, or dart,
In the King's train of Hungary,
    At hunting of the hart.
Past middle life—gray-haired—of face
    Swart from an orient sun—
Was never wight so lacked of grace
    As this stout champion.
Now—signal of accepted gage—
    He strikes with ready lance
Sir Gawen's shield, intent to wage
    Combat at utterance.

At signal of a bugle blast,
    Sharp and of sudden sound,

9*

The knights set forward, fiery fast,
    And met in middle ground.
Sir Gawen struck Sir John Cathore
    And bore his helm away—
But stout Sir John so rudely bore,
    That down went Gawen's gray:
Down went he wildly overthrown
    Before the stroke of force—
Down went he with a horrent groan,
    That grim and ancient horse.
His lady's cry reached Gawen's ear,
    Above the sounding strife:
That piercing cry, so wild to hear,
    Has nerved him into life.
From saddle-tree leapt John Cathore,
    But ere he touched the sand,
Sir Gawen stood the knight before,
    His good sword in his hand.
Now foot to foot, and hand to hand,
    The champions will contend:
By dint of honest blow of brand,
    The best will win his end.

But first Sir Gawen doffed, and threw
　　His knightly helm away—
Still to his fame, and honour, true,
　　However fare the day.
At vantage it were base to fight,
　　And helmless is Sir John ;
But now the knights in equal plight
　　To battle dire press on.

Sir John smote first, but with a bound
　　Sir Gawen shunned the blow,
And giving ground, and taking ground,
　　About the lists they go.
On young Sir Gawen's flowing hair,
　　And bright and manly brow—
On John Cathore's gray pow, half bare,
　　The level sun shines now.
Sir Gawen saw the flight so fast
　　All of the golden sun,
And lowly said, " This trial past,
　　And more than life is won."

His heart of valour seized the thought,
  Enflamed anew thereby,
And the bold youth his battle fought,
  Intent to win or die.

With blows, and thrusts, that seek a door
  At every rivet fine,
They fight until Sir John Cathore
  Bleeds like a cask of Rhine.
Griesly and grim have waxed his looks,
  Right hotly mounts his ire,
Rebuke of steel he badly brooks—
  His one eye glows like fire.

Be wary, Gawen—mind thy life!
  Sir John comes stormily.
" Close stroke of sword shall end this strife"—
  In stormy tone quoth he.
Down fell his blows like iron hail,
  With clangour loud and dread;
They struck the fire from Gawen's mail,
  They gleamed about his head.

With bound, and ward, and ready guard,
  Sir Gawen held his own,
While to and fro all saw them go—
  Sir Gawen and Sir John.
But now, forsooth, the sturdy youth,
  Sir Gawen, onset makes;
With brand or spear, the truth is clear,
  He gives as well as takes.
From first sweep of Sir Gawen's blade
  Sir John his safety found—
The next blow that Sir Gawen made,
  Down went he to the ground:
Down went Sir John with cloven brow,
  And nevermore to rise.
And Gawen Bolton, victor now,
  Is winner of the prize!
Peace to the soul of John Cathore:
  A bolder cavalier,
Or better captain, never bore
  His fortune on his spear.

With John Cathore cast down, and slain,
Ended the jousts of Bar-by-Seine.

And Charles, the regent, now will say
Who bears the lovely prize away.
Fronting the sunset's purple pride,
And hill tops with the glory dyed,
Charles watches, from his steed, to see
The burning disk sink utterly.
With the last flicker of its beams,
Dying amongst surrounding gleams,
He dropped his baton from his hand,
And forth bade good Sir Gawen stand.
" Brave knight," he said, " we do decree
All honours of this day to thee—
A chaplet for thy gallant head,
A countess for thy marriage bed.
This say we now—hereafter more.
Thy brows—and manlier never wore
Love's garland, won in front of death—
Will now receive the victor's wreath.
Haply—and, by our faith, we guess
So much—the lady's great distress,
Whereof the recent show made all
Condemn the good Lord Reyneval,

Will yield, in somewhat, when she finds
How frank and bold a brow she binds.
We know not of that shrewd surmise
Which speaks thy favour in her eyes;
But sure the countess, soon or late,
Will find contentment in her fate,
Nor rue this wooing of the sword
If gallant heart makes loving lord."

Sir Gawen, at his lady's feet,
Bends, harking to her words so sweet—
Some words of course, and which alone
Take meaning from their trembling tone.
But now her little hand, so fair,
Touches his brow, and lingers there.
Place, and that presence, speak him nay,
But Gawen wins the hand away,
And seals it to his lips, the while
The countess chides him with a smile.

The formal truth is clearly told
In the good chronicle of old,

How nuptial rites, and feasts, attended
By pomp and ceremony splendid,
Followed the jousts; how by decree
Watchful in points of fealty,
Sir Gawen, with his lady's hand,
Gained stately castles, gold and land;
And, with the rest, in fair requital
Of worthy deeds, a lordly title.
Such was his meed; and never one
Of the great counts of Rousillon
Such honour to his honours gave
As Gawen—gentle, truthful, brave,
Since the proud founder of their line,
With bands Franconian, crossed the Rhine.

GEOFFREY TETENOIRE.

THE Lady Jane, with urgent train,
    Comes trooping into Paris:
Her milk-white mule seems very proud
    Beneath the load he carries—
And, reason good, for fairer dame,
    Than lovely Lady Jane,
Is not between the Norman lands
    And mountain line of Spain.

The Lady Jane of Ventadore
    Is irritant of mood,
The dame is but a fugitive
    Before a robber rude;
Tetenoire, the Free Companion,
    Is master of her lands,

10

And castle strong, by hardy wrong,
    And holds them with his bands.

Thus is it that the Lady Jane
    Comes trooping into Paris—
Reining the little mule, so proud
    Beneath the load he carries.
Here may she be at liberty,
    And wisely meditate,
The wrong which she has undergone
    In pride, and in estate.

The countess came at June's sweet end,
    And, on an autumn day,
The County Gaston sought her side,
    His suit of love to pay :
" For thy dear love, all price above,
    And for thy hand so fair,
If win I may, sweet lady, say,
    What service shall I dare ?"

The yielding dame made answer then :
    " The whisper of a lute,

Were not so dear a sound to hear,
   As this thy gentle suit.
But, like the dame who bade her lord
   Leap down, and win her glove
From forth a lion's jaws, I bind
   A service to thy love.

Five years I dwelt, a widow lorn,
   In Castle Ventadore;
Tetenoire the Breton drove me forth,
   And wronged me much and sore;
If thou wilt slay the robber vile,
   And bring his head to me,
I freely vow, Sir Count, that thou,
   Shalt have my hand for fee."

     *   *   *   *

It was the County Gaston
   Drew on to Ventadore,
His men-at-arms behind him,
   His trumpeters before;
And by his side did proudly ride
   Sir Anthony Bonlance,

A sweet Parisian gentleman
  Of dainty countenance.
Between St. Flour and Ventadore,
  Fair in a forest glade,
The county rides, at stately pace,
  Before his cavalcade.
The autumn leaves, the count perceives,
  Have caught a beauty rare,
As if the rays of lovely days
  Had been entangled there.

And the near hills are ringing
  With merry songs and sweet—
The birds are piping merrily
  The early day to greet:
The early day, for on their way
  As forth the riders pass,
The sparkling dews, which night renews,
  Are bright on tree and grass.

Some gentle praise of nature
  The gallant count was saying,

When he was ware of horsemen near—
   He heard their chargers neighing.
And then he spurred his good steed up
   A near acclivity,
From whose broad top a loving eye
   A lovely land might see.

But not upon the beauty rare
   Of that most lovely land,
The county gazed—beyond the hill
   He saw an armed band :
A band, I ween, fair to be seen,
   Of mail-clad cavaliers,
Holding their way, in close array,
   With sunlit helms and spears.

Lord Gaston's hand waved brief command,
   And straight an Auvergne guide
Obeyed his signal, from the troop,
   And galloped to his side.
" Now who be they on yonder way ?
   Look freely and declare."

10*

Whereto the guide in haste replied,
   "The man you seek is there.

"For mark you not the litter borne
   Amidst the armed band?
They call it Geoffrey's battle-horse
   In all this southern land.
The robber bold is waxing old,
   And therefore travels so."
Then said the lord, "By my good sword!
   I joy so much to know."

And now he wheels his champing steed,
   And hurries from the height,
And joins his willing men-at-arms,
   And orders them aright.
"The enemy rides here," quoth he,
   "Beneath us on the plain,
In bold array, athwart our way,
   His castle hold to gain."

Tetenoire was wending on his route,
   So in his litter borne,

When, from the wooded height above,
   Rang out a bugle horn.
And with the sound, shaking the ground,
   Rushed down the charging horse—
With level spears, the cavaliers
   Came thundering on their course.

Grim Geoffrey raised his head and gazed,
   Expectant of the shock,
And laughed to see its fury break
   Like sea-foam on a rock.
" These lords," quoth he, right scornfully,
   " Misjudge me overmuch,
They pounce as if my eagle brood
   Were quarries for their clutch."

And then his dark, keen eye did mark
   Lord Gaston's haughty crest,
Where, chafed and baffled, to and fro
   He rode amongst the rest.
Intent the gallant county seemed
   To rally back his host,

Like one whose courage would regain
 Some rose of honour lost.

" Give me a cross-bow in my hand,
 And place a bolt therein"—
Grim Geoffrey said—" and bend the bow,
 And let the bolt be keen."
And then he scanned the county's band,
 And bade his own hold place—
A perilous smile was fierce the while
 Upon his ancient face.

As leant he on his litter's side,
 An old and feeble man,
With raven locks so wonderful
 Above his visage wan,
And peered with keen and ferret eyes—
 So subtil in their guile—
You would have said a common wrath
 Was kinder than his smile.

He raised the cross-bow to his aim,
 And then with sudden twang,

The bolt flew forth, and angrily
    Upon its journey sang.
The sharp bolt flew so swift, and true,
    That, ere a man might speak,
It smote the County Gaston
    Betwixt the eye and cheek.

Ah, ill betide the bowyer's craft,
    That shaped that bolt so true!
And ill betide the heart of pride,
    From whose fierce will it flew!
The county tottered on his horse,
    His brain span round and round,
And then he lost his rein, and fell
    A dead man to the ground.

Sir Anthony scarce stayed to see
    The County Gaston slain,
But turned to face the homeward hill,
    And urged his horse amain.
Now, by my troth, Sir Anthony
    Will surely win the race!

His knighthood claims, and holds, the van—
 Behind him bursts the chace.

Old Geoffrey in his litter lies,
 And marks his armed men
Come trooping back, in scattered groups,
 To win his side agen.
" Now who be these—our enemies—
 Who dare abroad to ride,
For foolish enterprise of arms,
 In this our country-side ?"

In answer to his master's quest,
 A griesly wight and strong
Came leading, through the merry crowd,
 A captive, by a thong.
Lashed like a hound—his fine arms bound—
 Came pale Sir Anthony.
The hapless plight of that fine knight
 Was very sad to see.

" This gentleman"—his captor said—
 " Was riding with the rest,

And, yea indeed! he led the race—
   His charger was the best.
But as he rode so terribly
   Upon his dapple gray,
The good beast stumbled at a ditch,
   And left him by the way."

Sir Anthony is tremulous,
   For he is troubled sore :
Right awful are the icy looks,
   Of him of Ventadore.
Quoth Geoffrey, " Speak the truth, and show
   What errand brought you here."
And, quakingly, Sir Anthony
   Made all the truth appear.

" Who seeks my head had well beware,"
   The Breton sternly said,
"Lest, groping in the lion's den,
   He lose his own instead."
Then, lowering darkly on the knight,
   He deigned to say no more,

But bade his trumpets lead the way
   En route for Ventadore.

    *   *   *   *

In a proud hall Parisian,
   With jewels quite a-blaze,
The Countess Jane was leading down
   The stately Polonaise,
When, like a discord, in the midst
   Of music proud, and dance,
In way-worn plight, stalked in the knight
   Sir Anthony Bonlance.

His beard defiled, his locks so wild,
   His garb in disarray—
Ah! can it be Sir Anthony,
   Who went so proud away?
A servitor behind him glides,
   And bears, as all may see,
A little casket, richly wrought
   Of gold and ebony.

" I bought my freedom at a price,"
   So said the haggard knight,

" Dearer than gold in red merks told—
    And I must pay aright
That ransom now, or break a vow
    Wherewith my soul is bound."
His sad, dark mien, and words, I ween,
    Have hushed the music's sound.

He came before the Countess Jane—
    Forlorn Sir Anthony !
And muttered, " I am sworn to bear
    This casket unto thee."
So said the haggard knight, and placed
    The casket in her hands ;
And she, in marvel at his words,
    Unclasped the golden bands.

Ah ! God and all good saints support
    The stricken Lady Jane !
Within is County Gaston's head—
    A bow-bolt in the brain !
She lost the casket from her hands—
    Out rolled the gory head—

And Lady Jane, with wandering arms,
   Fell down as fall the dead.

  *   *   *   *

A convent crowns a gentle hill
   Above the bounding Rhone,
And to its shades, for health of soul,
   The Countess Jane is gone:
A sister of that holy house,
   Her griefs of earth are dead—
But, in her dreams, the sister sees
   A casket and a head.

[IN the three following poems, Froissart, from whom I have faith-fully taken them, is made to address the reader directly. They are put into this shape to retain the pleasant pedantry about Acteon in the conclusion of Sir Peter of Bearn, and also the general naive cre-dulity of the good knight and his gossips, which makes a principal part of the charm of the prose chapters.

The reader may censure these poems, dealing in a low and homely order of the marvellous, as trivial in subject, and no fulfil-ment of the promise involved in the undertaking to versify portions of a history abounding in narratives of heroic and chivalric action. If he can find no good artistical reason for my grouping such ballads as a relief to the Master of Bolton and Geoffrey Tetenoire—poems full of martial narrative—he will please recollect (what my preface declares) that Orthone, Sir Peter of Bearn, and Our Lady's Dog, are but three out of many ballads, upon various subjects, already roughly written: and that they are by no means designed to be considered, in themselves, a fulfilment of the promise of my title page.

Gaston, Earl of Foix, at whose magnificent court Sir John learned these stories, seems to have been a great favourite with him. His account of the earl's appearance and mode of living is readable enough for quotation.

" Sir Espange de Lion went to the castle to the earl, after sunset, and found him in his gallery, for he had but recently dined ; for the earl's custom was to rise at noon and sup at midnight : the knight informed him of my arrival, and I was immediately sent for to my lodging at the Moon. When the earl saw me, he made me good cheer. * * * The acquaintance between me and the earl was because I had brought with me a book, which I had formed at the suggestion of Winceslaus of Bohemia, Duke of Luxembourg and Brabant, which book was called the Meliader, containing all the songs, ballads, rondeaus, and virelays, which the worthy duke had made in his time; and this book the earl was glad to see, and often I read therein to him, and while I read there was none durst speak a word. * * * This Earl Gaston of Foix was then fifty-nine years of age: and though I have seen many knights, kings, princes, and others, I never saw any of so fine a figure; his visage fair, sanguine, and smiling, his eyes gray and amorous, where he chose to set his regard: in every thing he was so perfect, that he cannot be praised too much: he loved what ought to be beloved, and hated what ought to be hated. He said many orisons daily; a nocturn of the psalter, matins of our Lady, of the Holy Ghost, and of the cross, and dirge every day: he gave five florins in small sums at his gate to poor folks for the love of God; he was generous and courteous in gifts; he loved hounds of all beasts; winter and summer he loved hunting. * * * He kept coffers in his chamber out of which he would often take money to give to lords, knights, and squires, for none ever left him without some present. * * * He would converse familiarly with all men; he was short in counsel and answers: he had four secretaries, ever ready at his rising without being called. At midnight when he came out of his chamber into the hall to supper, he had ever before him twelve torches burning, borne by twelve varlets. * * * The hall was ever full of knights and squires, and many other tables were prepared for any to sup who pleased; none spoke to him at his table unless he were called: his meat was usually wild fowls, the legs and wings only; * * * he would have songs sung before him; he was pleased at seeing humorous tricks performed at his table, and when he had seen them he would send them to the other tables. Before I came to his court I had been at the courts of many kings, princes, dukes, earls, and great ladies, but never in any that pleased me so much : and there were none who took more delight in deeds of arms than the earl did : there were seen in his hall, chamber, and court, knights and squires of honour going up and down, and talking of arms and amours: all honour was found there, and tidings from every realm and country might be heard there ; for out of every country there was resort on account of the valour of the earl. In this manner the Earl of Foix lived.''

At Ortaise, enjoying the favour of this great earl, Froissart meets with the Bastot Maulion, and Ernalton of Pine, who are very willing to gossip with so distinguished a clerk.]

11*

ORTHONE.

IT was the Bastot Maulion
   Who told this tale to me,
At Ortaise, by an ingle side,
   In gossip frank and free,
At the good hostel of the Moon,
   Where I sometime attended
The will of Gaston Earl of Foix,
   That potent lord, and splendid.

The Lord Corasse—the Bastot said—
   Had taken on his hands
Feud with a Catalonian clerk,
   Who sought to tithe his lands;
And dealt so rudely by the priest
   That he was fain to fly—
For the lord's wrath had put his life,
   He deemed, in jeopardy.

But ere the priest went forth, he came
    And yielded to the lord,
In formal wise, the cause of feud ;
    And then, at parting word,
Quoth he, " Corasse, your greater strength
    Has robbed me of my right :
I yield not to your argument,
    But only to your might."

" Ah, Master Martin !" said the lord,
    " I care not for your rage ;
Free living shall you never have
    From my fair heritage."
" So much I know ;" the clerk replied,
    " You violate the laws ;
But, swift as may be, I will send
    A champion of my cause.

" And he shall deal so by your peace,
    That you will sorely rue
That you have borne against the right,
    And robbed me of my due."

And, with such words, the angry clerk
　　Departed on his way:
The baron never saw him more
　　From forth that summer day.

Three nights thereafter, Lord Corasse
　　Lay quietly abed,
When, suddenly, the castle rung
　　With wondrous sounds and dread;
A clatter in the kitchens—
　　A thunder on the stair—
And shrillest voices screaming
　　Around it in the air.

The Lord Corasse sate up, and stared,
　　And seemed in trouble sore;
Then heard unmannered knocking
　　All at his chamber door.
His lady drew the curtains
　　In fear about her head,
But to his sword, reached forth the lord,
　　And, full of courage, said—

" Now who be ye who thunder so ?
    Pray let your names be shown."
And at the word, reply he heard,
    " They call my name Orthone."
" Orthone," replied the baron,
    " Who sent you here to me?"
" Your enemy, the Spanish clerk,
    Whose work I do"—quoth he.

" Orthone," said on the baron stout,
    " A beggar like the clerk
Will give you little thanks, or wage,
    For moiling at his work :
I pray you be my servant !"—
    With this the clamour ceased,
And Orthone said, " So let it be—
    I weary of the priest."

Thereafter Orthone served the lord,
    Invisible to him ;
Would seek his chamber nightly,
    When lights were burning dim,

And bring him news of distant lands,
    Of battle-field, and court ;
Did never post so little cost,
    Or bear such swift report.

One day the baron came to join
    A banquet at Ortaise,
And some loose speech of his did strike
    Earl Gaston with amaze.
" Brother !" quoth he, " how may it be—
    This thing thou dost declare—
Unless thou hast a messenger
    To fly upon the air ?"

And then the baron answer made,
    For he was glad with wine,
And told the earl the story—
    Who thereof did opine
As of a marvel deep, and said,
    " If ever thou hast seen
This messenger, in any shape,
    Pray tell me of his mien."

" I have not seen him," said Corasse,

   " Small use it were to see;

Sufficient that he comes, and goes,

   And serves me faithfully."

Then said the earl, " When next he comes,

   I pray thee bid him show

What look he wears—what shape he bears—

   So much I fain would know."

The Lord Corasse is now abed,

   And merry Orthone seeks

His side again, and plucks his ear,

   And toys upon his cheeks.

" Orthone—Orthone !" said Lord Corasse—

   " Good servant, prithee, show

What look you wear—what shape you bear—

   So much I fain would know."

" Sir," said Orthone, " I plainly see

   That you are bent to lose

A willing servant: but, for once,

   I grant the thing you choose.

Whatever, when you leave this bed,
    Your eyes first rest upon—
Observe it well, for certainly
    That thing will be Orthone."

The sun is shining yellowly,
    And dazzles on the bed ;
And Lord Corasse laughs loud to see
    His lady hide her head.
He sits upright, and laughs, and peers
    Around him everywhere,
But he may mark no living thing,
    No matter how he stare.

Uprose he then, and placed his foot
    Out on the rushes, strewn
So soft upon his chamber floor—
    Nor saw he yet Orthone.
But as he puts his foot abroad,
    A quick keen tickle goes,
Athwart the sole, and tingles
    Betwixt the wincing toes.

And as his foot he lifted,
   A single straw fell down,
And rested not, but skipped about,
   Over the rushes brown,
With somersets, and other feats—
   The like, man never saw,
And Lord Corasse looked on, and said,
   " The devil is in the straw."

But never deemed the Lord Corasse
   That he had seen Orthone ;
That day went by, he sought his bed
   When as its toils were done ;
And, at the middle watch of night,
   Orthone drew nigh again,
And plucked the baron by the ear,
   And plucked the counterpane.

" Orthone—Orthone !" his master said,
   " You err in coming here ;
You broke that promise made to me—
   So much is surely clear."

" I made a promise," said Orthone,
     " And truly held thereby :
The tumbling straw, whose feats you saw,
     That little straw was I."

" Ah !" quoth the lord, " I deemed the straw
     Was surely out of nature :
But prithee take some other form
     Of greater bulk and stature."
And so, again, the voice has said,
     " What first you look upon,
Observe it well, for certainly
     That thing will be Orthone."

The baron rose up with the sun,
     And looking up and down—
Now here, now there—and everywhere—
     Saw but the rushes brown,
And oaken stools, and cabinets—
     The room's appurtenances :
No semblance of his servant met
     His shrewd and roving glances.

Then to a lattice broad, he stept,
    And cast it open wide ;
And, looking down upon the court,
    He presently espied
A gaunt wild-sow, with ears, I trow,
    As long as of a hound,
And bristled back, and loathly dugs
    That trailed upon the ground.

The baron shouted to his men—
    It moved him so to see
That loathly beast—and bade them loose
    His bandogs speedily.
The mastiffs came out ramping,
    But eager-eyed and mute,
They snuffed the air, and flew to tear,
    And yell around the brute.

The wild-sow never tarried
    For bay, or roaring chace,
But gave a cry unearthly,
    And vanished from the place.

And then the baron knew the beast
    Was certainly Orthone,
And turned within, lamenting
    The thing that he had done.

Quoth he, " It would be merely just
    If Orthone left me now—
But certainly I deemed the beast
    Was but a loathly sow."
That night Corasse lay long awake,
    But lay awake in vain :
Orthone came not, and truly,
    He never came again.

So said the Bastot Maulion,
    And I have given his story
Fair place amongst my braver tales,
    Of policy and glory.
If it be true, or haply false,
    So much I cannot say :
But mysteries as great surround
    Our life by night and day.

SIR PETER OF BEARN.

I MET the knight Sir Ernalton
    In those right pleasant days,
When, in attendance on the earl,
    I tarried at Ortaise.
A wise and worthy knight was he—
    Sir Ernalton of Pine*—
And pleasant converse oft we held
    Above our cups of wine.

Sir Ernalton had much to say
    Whereof I loved to learn,
And once, it chanced, the converse turned
    Upon the knight of Bearn.

---

* I have given the English pronunciation to this name, as to most of the French names in these poems. In this I follow Lord Berners—if any evidence of pronunciation may be drawn from the various and capricious spelling of the old translator.

No man was near, our speech to hear,
 And we were frank with wine,
And therefore freely spake my friend,
 Sir Ernalton of Pine.

Quoth he, " The king, Don Pedro, slew,
 Some twenty years ago,
The Count of Biscay, for a cause
 Of which I nothing know.
His daughter, Lady Florens, fled
 To seek Earl Gaston here,
And came in grief before the earl,
 And made her story clear.

" Earl Gaston heard her grievous tale
 With generous concern,
And matched her with his kinsman young,
 The gallant knight of Bearn.
Sir Peter found sufficient art
 To quell his lady's tears,
And happily, as man and wife,
 They lived for many years.

" Now comes my tale : ten months ago,
   One pleasant winter morn,
The knight from Languedudon rode
   To hunt, with hound and horn ;
And it befell that in a dell,
   That most unlucky day,
The hounds of good Sir Peter brought
   A mighty boar to bay.

" Sir Peter heard their yells from far,
   And rode the greenwood fast :
And, drawing on, espied the boar—
   A monster fell and vast.
His fiery eyes, and foaming tusks
   Were fearful to be seen,
As in his wrath he ripped the dogs,
   And slew them on the green.

" ' Now, by St. Hubert !' said the knight,
   ' This thing must have an end :
It seems but pastime to the boar
   My gallant dogs to rend.'

And then he urged his horse amain,
   And dashed, in full career,
To bring that battle to an end
   With one true stroke of spear.

" But coming near, his charger swerved,
   And would not front the beast,
Whereat, I trow, Sir Peter's wrath
   Was mightily increased.
' Ah, craven !' quoth he to his horse,
   ' Dost thou so fail thy lord ?'—
And, leaping from his seat, he drew
   His trusty Bordeaux sword.

" An hour the knight waged battle hot,
   Against his foaming foe,
And sought his life with utmost skill
   Of cunning stab and blow.
An hour he fought, and verily
   The mighty boar he slew :
And, standing by the carcass vast,
   His merry bugle blew.

" His servants of the hunt came in,
   And they were in amaze,
And scrutinized the monster fell
   With wonder in their gaze.
' This boar,' said they, ' is sure the same
   That, twenty years ago,
Just here, in this same dell, alarmed
   Our lady's father so.'

" ' What say you ?' said the knight of Bearn,
   And then an aged wight
Came forth before the rest, and made
   Free answer to the knight ;
' Just twenty years ago,' quoth he,
   ' In this same month, and day,
The count, our lady's father, brought
   A boar like this to bay.

" ' And pressing hard upon the beast,
   In this green valley here,
Some devil's voice came suddenly,
   And strangely, to his ear.

Whether it came from ground, or air,
   Our lord could never tell:
But certainly the voice he heard—
   And others heard as well.

" ' *Why woundest thou a creature weak,*
   Whose comfort harms thee not?
The cruel shall die cruelly—
   Such were the words, I wot;
And, with their sound, the churning boar
   Passed free of spear and sword:
Within a year Don Pedro slew
   Our well-beloved lord!'

" ' Gramercy,' quoth Sir Peter then,
   ' My dame's unhappy sire
By the mere battle, proved the beast
   No better than a liar.
A hind may be a creature weak—
   Not so this giant boar:
But, certes, if he ever spake,
   The beast will speak no more!'

" Then back to Languedudon rode
  The knight, his halls to win,
Leaving the strongest of his train
  To bear the wild boar in ;
And when the men had cast their load
  Upon the pavèd court,
Sir Peter called his dame to see
  The trophy of his sport.

" Fair Lady Florens left her bower,
  And came forth readily,
And with a smile upon her face,
  The slaughtered boar to see :
But when she saw the gory beast,
  Her face grew wondrous pale,
And, lifting up her lily hand,
  She sought her eyes to veil.

" But presently she put away
  Her white hand from her eyes,
And freely gazed, and mused as one
  Who deals with mysteries.

Sometimes she mused, then wended back
    Her lonely bower to seek—
Her right hand pressed upon her breast,
    Her left upon her cheek.

" A lonely hour she passed in bower,
    Then came, with honeyed word,
And face quite cunning in its smiles,
    And thus addressed her lord:
' I owe a vow to good St. James,
    And, husband, I would fain
Take our dear daughter Adrienne,
    And journey into Spain.'

" Sir Peter heard his dame's request,
    And said, ' So let it be:'
And Lady Florens, with the word,
    Departed speedily.
From Castle Languedudon, forth
    She journeyed with her train;
And, by my troth, the wily dame,
    Came never back again.

" That night, when all were sound asleep,
   Sir Peter left his bed,
And seized his naked sword, and placed
   His basnet on his head ;
Fierce smote he right and left, and cried
   His sounding battle-cry :
I trow he deemed himself a-field,
   And in sore jeopardy.

" A little page, who shared his room,
   Fled from his blows aghast,
And reached the door, and flitted out,
   And made the strong bolt fast.
Long, from without, boy Gracien heard
   The knight that battle wage—
Heard wild Sir Peter's slashing blows,
   And cries of valiant rage.

" As sweet as summer did he seem—
   The gallant knight of Bearn !—
When, on the morrow, from his page,
   He came the truth to learn.

'Certes, dear boy,'—he smiled, and said—
    'I toiled to slay the boar,
And so my dreams were fever-wild:
    The thing will chance no more.'

" But, with the second night, once more
    Sir Peter left his bed,
And seized his naked sword, and placed
    His basnet on his head;
And shouted forth his battle-cry,
    And waged his fight amain;
While little Gracien, quite aghast,
    Escaped the room again.

" So passed his nights, until he pined;
    And now, as all may see,
By his wan looks, the gallant knight
    Is stricken mortally.
Ten months agone he slew the boar,
    And there are men who say
His wife, who augurs of his death,
    Can name his dying day.

" He here at Ortaise, with the earl—
　She with her friends in Spain—
Such thing, Sir John, should hardly be ;
　The wife should come again.
But she is versed in mysteries,
　Of necromantic art,
And such give cunning to the brain,
　But poison to the heart."

So said my friend Sir Ernalton :
　I mused his story's wonder—
It was a complex web, which I
　Might scarcely win asunder.
" Doubtless," I said at last, " the dame
　Knew more than she would say
Of the great beast Sir Peter slew
　On that unlucky day.

" Perchance, enlightened by her art,
　She knew the mighty boar
Was some fair knight, who rode that land
　In merry days of yore,

And angered some old forest god,
    Whose terrible decree
Thus brutalized the gentleman
    From his humanity.

" This seems quite strange—nay, wonderful—
    But, nathless, we are told
Of many cases similar
    In chronicles of old.
For instance—and a score of such
    My reading could impart—
The cavalier, young Acteon,*
    Was changed into a hart."

"Sir John"—said good Sir Ernalton—
    "Pray make that story clear:
I have not heard of Acteon,
    And much desire to hear."

---

* Shakspeare, and the old writers generally,—Lord Berners among the rest,—spell Actæon as I have done above; the delay on the diphthong, in pronunciation, is discordant in verse of rapid measure, and for that reason I have retained the ancient English spelling.

Then I replied, " This Acteon,
  Of whom you seek to know,
Was a right valiant gentleman,
  Who flourished long ago.

" The youth was fond of hound and horn,
  And all fair forest sport :
And, one day, riding in the woods—
  As chronicles report—
He roused a very noble hart,
  And pressed so eagerly
Upon that chase, that soon he lost
  His hounds and company.

" Holding his way for all that day,
  With speed and courage keen,
At setting of the sun he reached
  A meadow close and green—
A meadow with a pleasant brook,
  Shut in with beechen shades—
And caught Diana bathing there
  With all her snowy maids.

13*

" The goddess was confused enough,
    But, towering in her pride,
Refused her naked loveliness
    By any art to hide,
And chid her blushing girls, who sought,
    By crouching or by flying,
To shun the youth who sate his horse
    Their naked charms espying.

" ' Ah, hunter vile !'—Diana said—
    ' Whoever sent you here
Was not your friend, as presently
    Shall very well appear.
I will not that your tongue shall speak
    The secret of your eyes :
Your speech shall never put to shame
    Our maiden modesties.

" ' Take shape and likeness of the hart
    Which you have chased to-day !
It is my will : so let it be.'—
    And, sir, old writers say,

Young Acteon, with Diana's words,
    Assumed the horned looks
Of the wood-hart, whose natural love
    Is for the water-brooks.

" And finally, Sir Ernalton,
    The same old writers show,
That as the human quadruped
    Went plaining to and fro,
And gazing on his slender knees,
    His hounds came up with him,
And, urged on by the cruel maids,
    Soon tore him limb from limb.

" This is the tale of Acteon :
    And sad Sir Peter's dame,
I nothing doubt, from all you say,
    Knows more than she will name
Of that great boar her husband slew—
    And so, perhaps, should be
Excused, in somewhat, for her flight,
    And seeming cruelty."

" It may be," said Sir Ernalton,
 " That what you say is true :
But, sure, the dame deals cruelly
 Where tenderness is due.
The husband is a dying man,
 And, sir—I must maintain—
If he had slain St. Hubert's self,
 The wife should come again."

OUR LADY'S DOG.

THE Genoese had crossed the seas,
  And, with a mighty host,
Besieged a stately city,
  Upon the Moorish coast.
What time they lay at leaguer there,
  A strange event befell,
Whereof in this fair book of mine,
  I deem it good to tell.

It was at holy Easter—
  An hour before the day :—
The Christian host, with watches set,
  In heavy slumber lay,
When, pouring from the city's ports,
  The Paynim army came,
Led by the Moslem Afringor,
  A prince of valiant fame.

With night, and cloud, their march to shroud,
   And stealthy as the sea
When as its waters seek the shore,
   And gird it silently,
The enemies of God drew on
   To smite our slumbering host—
Drew on unwitnessed by the watch
   Asleep at every post.

But for a holy miracle,
   In mercy deigned to us,
The Cross had sunk that night before
   The Crescent orgillous.
But as the Paynim host drew on,
   A train of damsels bright,
Led by a lady fair of brow,
   Stood clearly in their sight.

And in her right hand, by a leash
   Of twisted silk and gold,
A milk-white dog, of mighty thews,
   The lady bright did hold.

Brave sentinel! with bay, and yell,
   The beast alarum made,
Until the Christian host were roused
   And gallantly arrayed.

The Christian knights see with amaze
   The lady and her train,
As visible as if by day,
   Before them on the plain:
And cross their brows in holy awe,
   As steadily they go
To do the lady's battle
   Against the Paynim foe.

The Moors, aghast, in terror passed
   To win back to their town;
But glaive and spear assailed their rear,
   And bore their strongest down.
And, it is said, the milk-white hound
   Was foremost in the fight,
And with his bristling jaws slew more
   Than any armed knight.

With rise of sun, and battle done,
　　No man saw longer there
The lady of the shining brow,
　　Or train of damsels·fair.
But the white hound, without a wound,
　　Snuffing the slaughter strode,
And came back to the Christian tents,
　　And with the host abode.

And then the men-at-arms who saw
　　The wonders of that night,
Called the brave beast OUR LADY'S DOG :—
　　For sure, the lady bright,
All said, was Mary Mother,
　　Who bare the blessed Lord,
And hates the race of Mahoun,
　　And loves the Holy Word.

And thenceforth did our Lady's dog
　　Keep constant watch and good,
And gentle nurture had he,
　　And sweet and dainty food;

Our Christians saw, with pious awe,
   The white crest of the hound,
As nightly, in his watchfulness,
   He went upon his round.

14

MISCELLANEOUS POEMS.

THE MOUNTAINS.

" Lowland, your sports are low as is your seat ;
The Highland games and minds are high and great."

TAYLOR'S BRAES OF MAR.

I.

THE axle of the Lowland wain
Goes groaning from the fields of grain :
The Lowlands suit with craft, and gain.

Good Ceres, with her plump brown hands,
And wheaten sheaves that burst their bands,
Is scornful of the mountain lands.

But mountain lands, so bare of corn,
Have that which puts, in turn, to scorn
The Goddess of the brimming horn.

14*

Go mark them, when, with tramp and jar,
Of furious steeds, and flashing car,
The Thunderer sweeps them from afar.

Go mark them when their beauty lies
Drooping and veiled with violet dyes,
Beneath the light of breathless skies.

No lands of fat increase may vie
With their brave wealth—for heart and eye—
Of loveliness and majesty.

II.

I stand upon an upland lawn;
The river mists are quite withdrawn—
It is three hours beyond the dawn.

Autumn works well! but yesterday
The mountain hues were green and gray:
The elves have surely passed this way.

With crimping hand, and frosty lip,
That merry elfin fellowship,
Robin and Puck and Numbernip,

Through the clear night have swiftly plied
Their tricksy arts of change, and dyed
Of all bright hues, the mountain side.

In an old tale Arabian,
Sharp hammer-strokes, not dealt by man,
Startle a slumbering caravan.

At dawn, the wondering merchants see
A city, built up gloriously,
Of jasper, and gold, and porphyry.

That night-built city of the sands
Showed not as show our mountain lands,
Changed in a night by elfin hands.

We may not find, in all the scene,
An unchanged bough or leaf, I ween,
Save of the constant evergreen.

The maple, on his slope so cool,
Wears his new motley, like the fool
Prankt out to lead the games of Yule.

Or rather say, that tree of pride
Stands, in his mantle many-dyed,
Bold monarch of the mountain side.

The ash—a fiery chief is he,
High in the highland heraldry :
He wears his proud robes gallantly.

Torch-bearers are the grim black pines—
Their torches are the flaming vines
Bright on the mountain's skyward lines.

The blushing dogwood, thicketed,
Marks everywhere the torrent's bed,
With winding lines of perfect red.

The oak, so haughty in his green,
Looks craven in an altered mien,
And whimples in the air so keen.

The hickories, tough although they be,
The chestnut, and the tulip-tree,
These too have felt the witchery.

The tree of life, and dusky pine,
And hemlock, swart and saturnine—
Staunch like a demon by his mine—

These still retain a solemn dress;
But, sombre as they be, no less
Make portion of the loveliness.

III.

Just now no whisper of the air
Awoke, or wandered, any where
In all that scene so wild and fair.

But hark! upborne by swift degrees,
Come forth the mountain melodies—
The music of the wind-tost trees.

And, startled by these utterings,
The parted leaves, like living things,
Skirl up, and flock on shining wings.

And, rising from the rainbow rout,
A hawk goes swooping round about—
And hark ! a rifle-shot, and shout.

The rifle of the mountaineer—
I know its tongue, so quick and clear—
Is out, to-day, against the deer.

Right hardy are the men, I trow,
Who build upon the mountain's brow,
And love the gun, and scorn the plough.

Not such soft pleasures pamper these
As lull the subtil Bengalese,
Or islanders of Indian seas.

A rugged hand to cast their seed—
A rifle for the red deer's speed—
With these their swarming huts they feed.

Such men are freedom's body guard;
On their high rocks, so cold and hard,
They keep her surest watch and ward.

Of such was William Tell, whose bow
Hurtled its shafts so long ago,
At red Morgarten's overthrow.

Of such was Arnold Winkelreid,
Who saved his fatherland at need,
And won in death heroic meed.

That deed will live a thousand years!
Young Arnold, with his Switzer peers,
Stood hemmed and hedged with Austrian spears.

No mountain sword might pierce that hedge,
But Arnold formed the Bernese wedge—
Himself, unarmed, its trusty edge.

His naked arms he opened wide,
"Make way for liberty," he cried,
And clasped the hungry spears—and died.

He *made* a gap for Liberty,
His comrades filled it desperately—
And Switzerland again was free.

IV.

But mark! on yonder summit clear,
Stands the bold hunter of the deer,
The rifle-bearing mountaineer.

From this far hill, we may not now
Mark the free courage of his brow,
Or the clear eyes, which well avow

The manly virtues of a heart,
Untrained to any baser art,
And bold to dare its lot and part.

But a strong vision may define,
His gaunt form's every giant line,
Motionless in the broad sunshine.

And his long gun we note and know—
That weapon dire of overthrow,
More terrible than Tell's true bow.

But mark again—his step descends;
And now his stately stature blends
With the vague path whereon he wends.

Bare is the gray peak where he stood—
Again the blue sky seems to brood
Over a lovely solitude.

V.

Our life on earth is full of cares,
And the worn spirit oft despairs
Under the groaning load it bears.

When such dark moods will force their way,
When the soul cowers beneath their sway,
Go forth as I have done to-day.

15

Boon nature is a foe severe
To pallid brow, and shadowy fear,
And lifts the fallen to valiant cheer.

Heed her good promptings—muse and learn—
And, haply, to thy toils return
With a clear heart, and courage stern.

FLORENCE VANE.*

I LOVED thee long and dearly,
   Florence Vane;
My life's bright dream, and early,
   Hath come again;
I renew, in my fond vision,
   My heart's dear pain,
My hope, and thy derision,
   Florence Vane.

The ruin lone and hoary,
   The ruin old,
Where thou didst hark my story,
   At even told,—

---

* This little poem, and "Young Rosalie Lee," were published some years ago, and met with more favour than I could ever perceive their just claim to. I am deterred by the success of these trifles from venturing upon the correction of some faults which I find in them—but which others may not consider faults. A reader's favourite verse might be *weeded* out in the process of correction.

That spot—the hues Elysian
    Of sky and plain—
I treasure in my vision,
    Florence Vane.

Thou wast lovelier than the roses
    In their prime ;
Thy voice excelled the closes
    Of sweetest rhyme ;
Thy heart was as a river
    Without a main.
Would I had loved thee never,
    Florence Vane !

But, fairest, coldest wonder !
    Thy glorious clay
Lieth the green sod under—
    Alas the day !
And it boots not to remember
    Thy disdain—
To quicken love's pale ember,
    Florence Vane.

The lilies of the valley
    By young graves weep,
The pansies love to dally
    Where maidens sleep;
May their bloom, in beauty vying,
    Never wane
Where thine earthly part is lying,
    Florence Vane!

15*

THE POWER OF THE BARDS.

WISDOM, and pomp, and valour,
  And love, and martial glory—
These gleam up from the shadows
  Of England's elder story.

If thou wouldst pierce those shadows
  Dark on her life of old,
Follow where march her minstrels,
  With music sweet and bold.

Right faithfully they guide us
  The darksome way along,
Driving the ghosts of ruin
  With joyous harp and song.

They raise up clearest visions,
  To greet us every where—

They bring the brave old voices
    To stir the sunny air.

We see the ships of conquest
    White on the narrow sea;
We mark from Battle Abbey,
    The plumes of Normandy.

We see the royal Rufus
    Go out the chase to lead—
Wat Tyrel's flying arrow—
    The dead king's flying steed.

We go with gallant Henry,
    Stealing to Woodstock bower,
To meet his gentle mistress,
    In twilight's starry hour.

We see Blondel and Richard,
    We hear the lays they sing;
We mark the dames adjudging
    Betwixt the bard and King.

We join the iron Barons,
    Doing that famous deed—
Wringing the great old charter
    From John at Runnymeade.

We ride with Harry Monmouth
    On Shrewsbury's bloody bounds ;
We hear the fat knight's moral,
    On Percy Hotspur's wounds.

We mark the bannered Roses—
    The red rose, and the white,
And Crookback's barded charger
    Foaming in Barnet fight.

We see bluff Harry Tudor,
    To royal Windsor ride,
With fair-necked Bullen reining
    A palfrey at his side.

We join Queen Bess, the virgin,
    And prancingly go forth,

To hold that stately revel
   At stately Kenilworth.

We join the ruder revels,
   Under the greenwood tree,
Where outlaw songs are chaunted,
   And cans clink merrily.

We join the curtal friar,
   And doughty Robin Hood,
And Scathelock, and the miller,
   At feast in green Sherwood.

We greet Maid Marian bringing
   The collops of the deer,
And pitchers of metheglin
   To crown the woodland cheer.

We lie down with the robbers
   At coming of the dark,
We rise, with their uprising,
   At singing of the lark.

And, blending with his matins,
    We hear the abbey chimes—
The chimes of the stately abbeys
    Of the proud priestly times.

*   *   *   *

And owe we not these visions
    Fresh to the natural eye—
This presence in old story—
    To the good art and high?—

The high art of the poet,
    The maker of the lays?
Doth not his magic lead us
    Back to the ancient days?

For evermore be honoured
    The voices sweet, and bold,
That thus can charm the shadows
    From the true life of old.

TO EDITH.

DEAR EDITH, I am pondering now,
With the sweet south wind on my brow,
And thoughtful eyes, which only see
The past, in sky, and grass, and tree.

Into the past I go to seek
The lustre of thy maiden cheek,
And all thy graces debonair—
I go to seek, and find them there.

Canst thou revisit, as I do,
The time wherein I learned to woo?
The time when, young in thought and years,
We learned love's lore of smiles and tears?

Our early love found early cure,
But, cousin mine, of this be sure—

In that fair time we loved as well
As stateliest lord and damosell.

If thou didst not, pray tell me why
Thy soul stood beckoning in thine eye*—
Playing the sweet mime with my own,
And evermore with mine alone?

If I loved not, why should it be
That, quickened by a thought of thee,
My spirit goes forth fiery fast
To meet thee in the radiant past?

Ah! break not in thine ignorance
The golden rule of that romance,
But let it hold thy riper age,
As mine, in happy vassalage.

---

* I find that this line is almost identical with one in a poem
addressed by Lord Carbery (1672) to his wife. My verses are
too flimsy to be meddled with, or I would put another in its
place.

As mine !—by Eros, to be free
From bondage of that memory,
Were but to wear a colder chain—
Were but to give my bliss for pain.

16

LIFE IN THE AUTUMN WOODS.

Summer has gone!
And fruitful autumn has advanced so far,
That there is warmth not heat in the broad sun,
And you may look with steadfast gaze upon
    The ardours of his car;
The stealthy frosts, whom his spent looks embolden,
    Are making the green leaves golden.

What a brave splendour
Is in the October air! How rich and clear—
How life-full, and all joyous! We must render
Love to the Spring-time, with its sproutings tender,
    As to a child quite dear—
But autumn is a noon, prolonged, of glory—
    A manhood not yet hoary.

I love the woods
In this best season of the liberal year;

I love to haunt their whispering solitudes,
And give myself to melancholy moods,
        With no intruder near;
And find strange lessons, as I sit and ponder,
        In every natural wonder.

        But not alone
As Shakspeare's melancholy courtier loved Ardennes,
Love I the autumn forest; and I own
I would not oft have mused as he, but flown
        To hunt with Amiens—
And little recked, as up the bold deer bounded,
        Of the sad creature wounded.

        That gentle knight,
Sir William Wortley, weary of his part,
In painted pomps, which he could read aright,
Built Warncliffe lodge—for that he did delight
        To hear the belling hart.
It was a gentle taste, but its sweet sadness
        Yields to the hunter's madness.

What passionate
And wild delight is in the proud swift chase!
Go out what time the lark, at heaven's red gate,
Soars joyously singing—quite infuriate
With the high pride of his place;
What time the unrisen sun arrays the morning
In its first bright adorning.

Hark the shrill horn—
As sweet to hear as any clarion—
Piercing with silver call the ear of morn;
And mark the steeds, stout Curtal, and Topthorn,
And Greysteil, and the Don—
Each one of them his fiery mood displaying
With pawing and with neighing.

Urge your swift horse
After the crying hounds in this fresh hour—
Vanquish high hills—stem perilous streams perforce—
Where the glades ope give free wings to your course—
And you will know the power
Of the brave chase—and how of griefs, the sorest,
A cure is in the forest.

Or stalk the deer :
The same red fires of dawn illume the hills,
The gladdest sounds are crowding on your ear,
There is a life in all the atmosphere ;—
Your very nature fills
With the fresh hour, as up the hills aspiring,
You climb with limbs untiring.

It is a fair
And pleasant sight, to see the mountain stag,
With the long sweep of his swift walk, repair
To join his brothers ; or the plethoric bear
Lying on some high crag,
With pinky eyes half closed, but broad head shaking,
As gad-flies keep him waking.

And these you see,
And, seeing them, you travel to their death,
With a slow stealthy step from tree to tree—
Noting the wind, however faint it be ;
The hunter draws a breath
In times like these, which he will say repays him
For all the care that waylays him.

16*

A strong joy fills—
A rapture far beyond the tongue's cold power—
My heart in golden autumn: fills and thrills!
And I would rather stalk the breezy hills—
Descending to my bower
Nightly by the bold spirit of health attended—
Than pine where life is splendid.

TO MY DAUGHTER LILY.

Six changeful years are gone, Lily,
   Since you were born, to be
A darling to your mother good,
   A happiness to me ;
A little, shivering, feeble thing
   You were to touch and view,
But we could see a promise in
   Your baby eyes of blue.

You fastened on our hearts, Lily,
   As day by day wore by,
And beauty grew upon your cheeks,
   And deepened in your eye ;
A year made dimples in your hands,
   And plumped your little feet,
And you had learned some merry ways
   Which we thought very sweet.

And when the first sweet word, Lily,
    Your wee mouth learned to say,
Your mother kissed it fifty times,
    And marked the famous day.
I know not even now, my dear,
    If it were quite a word,
But your proud mother surely knew,
    For she the sound had heard.

When you were four years old, Lily,—
    You were my little friend,
And we had walks, and nightly plays,
    And talks without an end.
You little ones are sometimes wise,
    For you are undefiled ;
A grave grown man will start to hear
    The strange words of a child.

When care pressed on our house, Lily,—
    Pressed with an iron hand—
I hated mankind for the wrong
    Which festered in the land ;

But when I read your young frank face,—
  Its meanings, sweet and good,
My charities grew clear again,
  I felt my brotherhood.

And sometimes it would be, Lily,
  My faith in God grew cold,
For I saw virtue go in rags,
  And vice in cloth of gold ;
But in your innocence, my child,
  And in your mother's love,
I learned those lessons of the heart
  Which fasten it above.

At last our cares are gone, Lily,
  And peace is back again,
As you have seen the sun shine out
  After the gloomy rain ;
In the good land where we were born,
  We may be happy still,
A life of love will bless our home—
  The house upon the hill.

Thanks to your gentle face, Lily !
　Its innocence was strong
To keep me constant to the right,
　When tempted by the wrong.
The little ones were dear to Him
　Who died upon the Rood—
I ask his gentle care for you,
　And for your mother good.

THE MURDER OF CORNSTALK.*

THE miller sate at his cabin door—
A man of seventy years and more;
It was old Michael Beattison,
The gray-beard miller of Crooked Run.

The summer boughs of a chestnut spread
Over his white and reverend head,

---

* The Shawnee chief Cornstalk, head of the great northern confederacy of tribes, was murdered by the whites at Point Pleasant in 1777. The circumstances attending his death are given faithfully in the poem. See Kerchival's Virginia Valley, and Howe's Virginia Collections. Crooked Run is a small stream near and running parallel with the Ohio; it empties into the Kanawha. On the strip between this little stream and the Ohio was fought the battle of Point Pleasant between the Virginians under Andrew Lewis and the warriors of the northern tribes led by Cornstalk—October, 1774. At the date of the murder—three years after the battle—Arbuckle was captain of the fort at Point Pleasant. Tradition and history represent the Cornstalk chief as the greatest and wisest of the great Indian "kings."

And, catching the west wind in their leaves,
Rustled against his cabin eaves.
The wind that stirred the lintel tree
Touched the old man tenderly.

Serene of look the miller sate
Erect in his wicker chair of state,
And now and then a smile would grace
The pleasant lines of his fresh hale face.
Was it because his earnest mill,
With merry clank, and clamour shrill,
Discoursed so well beneath the hill?
Or is it because some thought swells high
Of happy scenes in the time gone by?

The miller's hoary pow has store
Of frontier deeds, and Indian lore,
And he can show old times as well
As any written chronicle.

I, with another, crossed the green,
Saying, " Old gentleman, good e'en,"

And Michael, with fair courtesy,
Gave the good even back to me.
"Michael," I said, "my friend is taking
Notes for a good book he is making,
And much desires to hear you tell
The tale you bear in mind so well—
How the great sachem long ago
Was killed with Ellinipsico."

A happy man seemed Michael then.
"Good sirs," quoth he, "I was but ten,
When Cornstalk died; but older men
Have told me how the murder chanced.
My life is very far advanced,
But not enough that I should know,
Of things that chanced so long ago,
Like one who saw the very deed."

"Michael," I said, "there is no need
To parley so; pray tell the story."

Freely upspake the old man hoary,
"Sirs, I will tell what I have heard.

17

In seventy-seven some scouts brought word
That the great chief was coming down,
From his Chilicothe town,
To meet Arbuckle at the fort.
And shortly after this report
He came; myself was there that day,
For folk had come, from miles away,
In crowds to see the Shawnee king.
The Winnebago, Eagle-wing,
Came with him, for the two were friends,
And wrought together for their ends.
I saw them come, and can declare
What like of men the chieftains were.
The Shawnee was a man of care,
A grave, and quiet man, and old,
But upright in his gait, and bold,
And with a look about the eyes
Which said that he was good and wise.
He left his arms beyond the river,
And came up, like a sage lawgiver,
In flowing robes.   The Eagle-wing
Was younger than the Shawnee king,

But a great chief and orator.
The two had fought in seventy-four
On that same spot, and Cornstalk's look
Calm survey of the country took.
He raised his robes, and touched a scar,
And said some words of Dunmore's war,
And smiled—and then, with thoughtful port,
Entered the gateway of the fort.

" His words and voice were soft, and low,
But there were men at hand who said
That it was craft that they were so ;
For on the bloody day, and dread,
Of that great fight, when Lewis thinned
His lines, the old chief's cry rang out
As loud as any stormy wind ;
There was a tempest in his shout
That drowned the guns.   ' Be strong—be strong,'
Was Cornstalk's battle-cry, and long
The frontier bore its sound in mind.
Our women heard it in the wind

That swept the forests, bare and brown,
When autumn nights had settled down,
And fear sat by the chimney side ;
And hushed their children when they cried,
In wantonness of baby grief,
With stories of the Cornstalk chief.

" What drew the Shawnee to the fort,
Indeed I cannot well report.
Some said he came down as a spy—
If so he merited to die.
But others have it that he came—
And this seems truer—to proclaim
That the great northern tribes were won
By British arts, and he must run
With the strong stream, unless we brought
Sure aid to him—and such he sought.
This sounds more like the Shawnee king.
However, after counselling,
Our men—to make my story short—
Refused to let him leave the fort.

A month passed by.   The Eagle-wing,
Denied his freedom, seemed to pine;
But the stout-hearted Shawnee king—
They said who saw him—gave no sign
Of moodiness, but seemed to be
Careless of his captivity.
He kept his head, and heart, erect,
And, with courageous counsel, checked
The misery of his pining friend;
Saying, ' The oak should never bend'—
And to the white men—' We are here,
And helpless, but we have no fear;
I—weary and old and worn—am ready
To live or die.' His looks were steady—
Serene his voice—erect his head—
When valiant words like these he said.

" I said a long month passed away.
In the fifth week, one quiet day,
The Shawnee sachem, with a wand,
Was mapping, on a floor of sand,

17*

The winding rivers of the west.
Arbuckle, Stuart, and the rest
Were looking on, when suddenly
   The old chief paused with listening ear,
As one who catches some far cry,
   Then raised his face with pleasant cheer,
And smiled, and said that he had heard
' The whistle of a Shawnee bird.'
These words to Eagle-wing he said,
And left the hut with stately tread.

" He stept three steps beyond the door.
The river* passed with a solemn roar,
But over its sounds from the westward shore,
Where the dark-green boughs of the forest hung,
He heard a call in the Shawnee tóngue.
He shouted in turn—the voice replied—
And an Indian came to the water-side.
He looked on the current swift and clear,
For a little time, as a man in fear,
Then took to the stream like a mountain deer.

---

* The Ohio.

Sometime he waded, sometime he swam :
The chief looked on with a visage calm—
There was no light in his face to show
That he knew his son in the stream below,
His dear boy Ellinipsico.

". That night passed by ; the guard who kept
Watch on the hut where the Indians slept,
Heard the voices of father and son,
And their falling footsteps, one by one,
For an hour beyond the middle night—
Himself then fell asleep outright.
He said the words—in that strange sweet tongue—
Of the ancient chief, and the boy so young,
Were like some music—so soft they were.
The day came on serene and fair,
And, side by side, in the open air,
With moving lips, and steps most slow,
The white men saw them come and go—
Cornstalk and Ellinipsico.

" That day, at rising of the sun,
Gilmer, and Robin Hamilton

Had left the fort to stalk for deer
On the Kanawha's southern side.
It chanced some Delawares lurked near—
These crouching Delawares espied
The hunters, from their screen of grass,
And lay in wait, to let them pass,
Then fired upon them; Gilmer fell,
And the red devils, with a yell,
Leapt out, and rushed on Hamilton.
But Robin turned, and ran to win
The river-side—which soon he won,
And in his fear plunged headlong in.
His friends came swiftly to his aid,
And plucked him from the stream half dead,
Half drowned and terribly dismayed.

" His comrades heard the hunter's story,
With vengeful threats, and curses loud;
But at sight of the dead man, scalped and gory,
A very fiend possessed the crowd.
John Hall, a desperate man and bad,
Said with an oath, ' The Shawnee lad

Brought down these Indians when he came.'
The crowd was grass—these words were flame.
Awful and stern outbrake the cry,
' The Indians in the fort must die.'

" Arbuckle strove, but strove in vain,
The fury of the crowd to rein—
Its fierce intent of blood to check.
Right little did the miscreants reck
Of such entreaty or command.
John Hall, with rifle in his hand,
And a wild devil in his eye,
Menaced his captain for reply.

" Meanwhile the Indians sat alone,
Nor knew what fate came swiftly on ;
But Stuart broke in suddenly,
And warned them of the peril nigh.
The Winnebago glared around,
For refuge, but no refuge found,
And bent his dark brows to the ground.
The trembling Ellinipsico
His innocence essayed to show,

Saying, with utterance like a moan,
' Father, I came on my way alone.
My path was single in the wood.
Our people are white of the Long Knife's blood.'
But the great chief, the pale boy's sire,
Calmly arranged his wild attire ;
Courage and pride were in his face,
And he stood in his robes with a stately grace,
And spoke with an air of majesty—
' My son,' he said, ' fear not to die.
The Mighty Spirit who loves our race
Looked on my old age tenderly,
And sent my son to die with me.'

" The mob surged onward with a roar.
The bristling guns are at the door !
' What Manitou wills is for the best,'
The old chief said, and bared his breast.
A click of locks !—and the rifles tore
The sachem's very heart, and bore
His body, drenched with its spouting blood,
Far back from where in life it stood.

The poor boy Ellinipsico—
His eyes saw not that scene of wo.
The courage of his race had come
To nerve him for the martyrdom,
But his weak vision could not brave
The face of murder, and he gave
His young life to the sacrifice
With bending head and cowering eyes.
The Winnebago stood at bay,
And, bloody from brow to knee, contended ;
But his fierce life soon ebbed away,
And then the tragedy was ended.
And with it ends my old-world story."
So said, and sighed, the miller hoary.

My bookish friend—when he had done—
Gave thanks to Michael Beattison ;
And said such tales were worth the printing,
And, with some fair art in the minting,
Would pass as well as many told
In the high chronicles of old.

YOUNG ROSALIE LEE.

I LOVE to forget ambition,
 And hope, in the mingled thought
Of valley, and wood, and meadow,
 Where, whilome, my spirit caught
Affection's holiest breathings—
 Where under the skies, with me
Young Rosalie roved, aye drinking
 From joy's bright Castaly.

I think of the valley, and river,
 Of the old wood bright with blossoms;
Of the pure and chastened gladness
 Upspringing in our bosoms.
I think of the lonely turtle
 So tongued with melancholy;
Of the hue of the drooping moonlight,
 And the starlight pure and holy.

Of the beat of a heart most tender,
  The sigh of a shell-tinct lip
As soft as the land-tones wandering
  Far leagues over ocean deep ;
Of a step as light in its falling
  On the breast of the beaded lea
As the fall of the faery moonlight
  On the leaf of yon tulip tree.

I think of these—and the murmur
  Of bird, and katydid,
Whose home is the graveyard cypress
  Whose goblet the honey-reed.
And then I weep ! for Rosalie
  Has gone to her early rest ;
And the green-lipped reed and the daisy
  Suck sweets from her maiden breast.

18

LOVE AND BE KIND.

How hotly men will wrangle—
    One furious with another!
See how the strong hands mangle
    Some poor down-trodden brother.
Is this the lofty nature?
    Is this the lordly mind?
Can no poor human creature
    Love and be kind?

But if such strife be common,
    There still are nobler spirits
To rescue and illumine,
    The mould that man inherits.
Such, with the lamp of goodness,
    A tranquil pathway find,
Such, in the raging rudeness,
    Are gentle and kind.

Strive boldly, human brother—
    Not with your fellow-creature
But in self-war—to smother
    All growth of evil nature.
Be of the nobler spirits!
    Forgive, forget, be blind
To others' faults—not merits;
    Love and be kind.

Then, if it chance such yielding
    Invite the rude aggression—
If patience gives no shielding
    Against a base oppression;
Stand up, and dare the danger
    In armour manifold—
Defender, not avenger:
    Be strong and bold!

IMAGINARY ILLS.

I HAVE read of a man encompassed*
    By phantoms dire and grim ;
        In an ancient park,
        As the day grew dark,
They came about his pathway dim,
And with weird eyes encompassed him.

It was the Roundhead captain,
    The dreamer Harrison.
        With carnal might
        He strove to smite
The ghosts, that closed his blade upon
Like thin folds of a vapour dun.

---

* The reader will recollect the scene, in Woodstock, in which
the enthusiast Colonel Harrison does battle with his imaginary
enemies.

In such an armageddon
    Do not all mortals strive?
      Our timorous wills
      Create vague ills
Whereat we strike—but they survive
The many-spending blows we give.

Good friend! waste not your prowess
    Against such phantom woes.
      Be stout of heart,
      Bring courage, and art,
Against your real sorrows :—those
Are often vanquishable foes.

18*

Some sentences from Cary's Dante will afford a proper introduction to my translation of the famous story of Ugolino. Dante, conducted by Virgil, has reached the ninth round of the frozen circle, and there—

> " I beheld two spirits by the ice
> Pent in one hollow, that the head of one
> Was cowl unto the other ; and as bread
> Is ravened up through hunger, the uppermost
> Did so apply his fangs to the other's brain
> Where the spine joins it. Not more furiously
> On Menalippus' temples Tydeus gnawed
> Than on that skull and on its garbage he.
>   ' O thou! who showest so beastly sign of hate
> 'Gainst him thou preyest on, let me hear,' said I,
> ' The cause, on such condition, that if right
> Warrant thy grievance, knowing who you are,
> And what the colour of his sinning was,
> I may repay thee in the world above,
> If that, wherewith I speak, be moist so long.' "
>   Cary. Canto XXXII.—Inferno.

The " uppermost spirit" so entreated tells his story, which I translate.

STORY OF UGOLINO.

His reeking jaws the sinner raised at last,
  And wiped them grimly on the skull's vile hair,
Seeking to cleanse them of their fell repast,
  Then said: " Thy will obeying, I declare
The story of my woes.   If it may be
  That what I utter shall prove seed to bear
Fruit of eternal shame and infamy,
  To him, the traitor whom I mangle and tear,
Then will my earnestness speak weepingly.

" Who thou mayst be, or how art come beneath,
  I know not, but thou seemest Florentine
By thy sweet utterance.   I, or ere my death,
  Was County Ugolino; this malign
Damned spirit was Ruggieri.   Thou shalt hear,
  For reason strong my dire tale will assign,
Why in this place I neighbour him so near.—
  That trust in him wrought death to me and mine
Thou knowest and I need not make more clear.

" But what thou canst not know that will I tell—
  The ghastly secret of the Famine Tower !
Hear it, and judge thou if he loved me well.

  Mewed with my sons in that most horrible bower,
Which takes its title from our martyrdom,

  I watched the days creep onward, hour by hour,
Until my sense such watching did benumb ;

  Then slept I that ill sleep which hath the power
To lift the curtain from the time to come.

" I saw mine enemy—this one—bedight
  As master of the sport, go out to sweep
The Julian mountain that forbids the sight

  Of Lucca to the Pisan.   Up the steep,
His sons rode with him, ranging at his back ;

  The boys shrill-voiced, their sire with halloo deep,
Urged on the fury of lean dog and brach—

  Keen brutes and questing.   After that my sleep
Saw the fierce riders flagging on their track,

  And then their sides—tusk-rended—gape and weep.

" When as my sleep and dream were banished,
  Some voices in the darkness reached mine ear.

Sleeping, my children wept, and asked for bread.

    Right cruel art thou if thou hast no tear

At thought of my poor heart's foreboding load!

    Now had they wakened, and the hour drew near

Wherein it was the wont to dole us food,

    And each watched hungrily—but did appear

Some ghastly news, within himself, to bode.

" Then heard I harsh keys lock the outward gate

    O' the horrible tower: whence uttering not a word,

But staring on my murdered sons, I sate.

    I wept not—so all stone I was—but heard

My boys weep: then my little Anselm cried,

    ' Father, what ails thee?' and his wan face reared,

To read my looks.   I turned my face aside,

    And shed no tear—nor anywise appeared

A man of pangs, but dumb and leaden-eyed.

" And I sate so until a second sun

    Made glad the freedom of the outer air.

But when a faint beam trembled in upon

    Four faces, imaging my own dumb care,

On either hand, in agony, I bit.

   My sons, who, in that motion of despair,
Saw but the craving of a hunger fit,

   Cried, ' Father, thou didst give this flesh we wear,
Resume it in thy want, and eat of it.'

" And, not to make them sadder, thence I sate

   Holding my spirit in stillness.   Silently
Two days went by.   Ah, earth most obdurate!

   Why didst not ope on our great misery ?
The fourth day came, and Gaddo—my meek-eyed

   And best-loved Gaddo—sank and cried to me,
' Father, hast thou no help !'—and there he died.

   And plain as thou seest me, saw I the three,
Two days thereafter, fall down side by side.

" Thence I betook me, now grown blind, to grope

   Above them, and for three dark days made moan,
Calling upon the dead in wo, not hope ;

   Then hunger of my grief fell mastery won."

Here ending, Ugolino turned to hug
　　His skull, as a gaunt mastiff hugs a bone,
And, slavering fiercely as he fastened, dug
　　His teeth into its scalp, and fed thereon
With many a mangling grip, and sidelong tug.

Pisa! thou burning shame of all who be
　　Dwellers within that region of delight,
Where sweetest is the voice of Italy!
　　Since man is slow to punish thee aright—
May firm Capraia and Gorgona rise
　　From their isled roots, and dam to drowning height
The waves of Arno, till thy perishing cries
　　Prove that thou payest, to the last bloody mite,
Even pang for pang, thy debt of cruelties.

Thou vile! thou murder-fronted! what if fame
　　Reported that thy castles were betrayed
By that fierce sire? Doth it abate the shame
　　Leprous upon thee for his children dead?

Brigata, Hugo, and the sweet ones—twin

   In gentleness—of whom my song hath said:
If sin there were, how might these join therein?

   Thou modern Thebes! their very childhood made
These tender ones incapable of sin!

THE END.

The Romantic Tradition in American Literature

An Arno Press Collection

Alcott, A. Bronson, editor. **Conversations with Children on the Gospels.** Boston, 1836/1837. Two volumes in one.

Bartol, C[yrus] A. **Discourses on the Christian Spirit and Life.** 2nd edition. Boston, 1850.

Boker, George H[enry]. **Poems of the War.** Boston, 1864.

Brooks, Charles T. **Poems, Original and Translated.** Selected and edited by W. P. Andrews. Boston, 1885.

Brownell, Henry Howard. **War-Lyrics** and Other Poems. Boston, 1866.

Brownson, O[restes] A. **Essays and Reviews Chiefly on Theology, Politics, and Socialism.** New York, 1852.

Channing, [William] Ellery (The Younger). **Poems.** Boston, 1843.

Channing, [William] Ellery (The Younger). **Poems of Sixty-Five Years.** Edited by F. B. Sanborn. Philadelphia and Concord, 1902.

Chivers, Thomas Holley. **Eonchs of Ruby:** A Gift of Love. New York, 1851.

Chivers, Thomas Holley. **Virginia;** or, Songs of My Summer Nights. (Reprinted from *Research Classics,* No. 2, 1942). Philadelphia, 1853.

Cooke, Philip Pendleton. **Froissart Ballads,** and Other Poems. Philadelphia, 1847.

Cranch, Christopher Pearse. **The Bird and the Bell,** with Other Poems. Boston, 1875.

[Dall], Caroline W. Healey, editor. **Margaret and Her Friends.** Boston, 1895.

[D'Arusmont], Frances Wright. **A Few Days in Athens.** Boston, 1850.

Everett, Edward. **Orations and Speeches,** on Various Occasions. Boston, 1836.

Holland, J[osiah] G[ilbert]. **The Marble Prophecy,** and Other Poems. New York, 1872.

Huntington, William Reed. **Sonnets and a Dream.** Jamaica, N. Y., 1899.

Jackson, Helen [Hunt]. **Poems.** Boston, 1892.

Miller, Joaquin (Cincinnatus Hiner Miller). **The Complete Poetical Works of Joaquin Miller.** San Francisco, 1897.

Parker, Theodore. **A Discourse of Matters Pertaining to Religion.** Boston, 1842.

Pinkney, Edward C. **Poems.** Baltimore, 1838.

Reed, Sampson. **Observations on the Growth of the Mind.** *Including,* **Genius** (Reprinted from *Aesthetic Papers,* Boston, 1849). 5th edition. Boston, 1859.

Sill, Edward Rowland. **The Poetical Works of Edward Rowland Sill.** Boston and New York, 1906.

Simms, William Gilmore. **Poems:** Descriptive, Dramatic, Legendary and Contemplative. New York, 1853. Two volumes in one.

Simms, William Gilmore, editor. **War Poetry of the South.** New York, 1866.

Stickney, Trumbull. **The Poems of Trumbull Stickney.** Boston and New York, 1905.

Timrod, Henry. **The Poems of Henry Timrod.** Edited by Paul H. Hayne. New York, 1873.

Trowbridge, John Townsend. **The Poetical Works of John Townsend Trowbridge.** Boston and New York, 1903.

Very, Jones. **Essays and Poems.** [Edited by R. W. Emerson]. Boston, 1839.

Very, Jones. **Poems and Essays.** Boston and New York, 1886.

White, Richard Grant, editor. **Poetry:** Lyrical, Narrative, and Satirical of the Civil War. New York, 1866.

Wilde, Richard Henry. **Hesperia:** A Poem. Edited by His Son (William Wilde). Boston, 1867.

Willis, Nathaniel Parker. **The Poems, Sacred, Passionate, and Humorous, of Nathaniel Parker Willis.** New York, 1868.